IT ALL STARTED
WITH LASAGNA

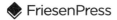 FriesenPress

Suite 300 - 990 Fort St
Victoria, BC, V8V 3K2
Canada

www.friesenpress.com

ISBN
978-1-5255-9698-8 (Hardcover)
978-1-5255-9697-1 (Paperback)
978-1-5255-9699-5 (eBook)

1. Business & Economics, Personal Success

Distributed to the trade by The Ingram Book Company

CONTENTS

IT ALL STARTED WITH LASAGNA

The Life Story of Peter Mercanti and His Ingredients for Business Success, Leadership and Happiness

FOREWORD BY: PAUL HENDERSON

My grandchildren with one on the way

DEDICATION

This book is dedicated to my mother, Iolanda Mancini, who planted in her children the seeds of kindness and generosity; my father, Giuseppe Mercante, who taught us the value of hard work and righteous living; my beautiful wife of fifty years, Gabriella Fernetti, who has guided and supported me every step of the way, and my three children, Daniella, PJ and Joey, and nine grandchildren, Michael, Nick, Marco, Francesco, Matthew, Gloria, Joseph, Savannah and Evangeline, who bring me more joy than all the riches the world has to offer.

The proceeds from the sale of this book will be donated to the Charity of Hope.

charityofhope.com

A MESSAGE FROM
THE FOUNDER AND CHAIRMAN

My mother taught us from a young age to be kind and generous. She would often say to us, "Do good for people and forget about it. Don't expect anything in return." No matter how meagre our life was, Mom would often say, "We are blessed."

The seeds for this charity were planted when George Lamparski, one of our handball teammates, approached our handball group and asked if we would donate money to buy boots and a coat for a young Polish immigrant girl. We were happy to donate. After doing this for a couple of years, we registered the Charity of Hope, operated by volunteers, allowing us to give one hundred percent of proceeds to children in our community who were in need. Being an immigrant myself, I could relate to the needs of new immigrants, especially the children who experience all kinds of challenges.

As CARSTAR President, I reached out to many of our suppliers, and they were happy to donate. This, combined with Carmen's organizing fundraising events and people's personal donations, ensured the money started to roll in. We offer two scholarships for high-school kids: The Spirit Award in memory of our brother Morris, who exemplified courage and grit in his battle with cancer, and the Better Man Award in memory of Tony DePaulo Jr. The Charity of Hope has granted wishes that have given hope to thousands of children, youth and their families since 1999. Everyone has the right to achieve their hopes and dreams!

We are blessed to have a phenomenal team of dedicated volunteers: My wife Roma, who does all the due diligence; my three daughters, Samantha, Jennifer and Lisa, who work hard making this charity a success; my brothers, Peter and Morris, who have always been there for us raising money and working hard; and our own enthusiastic and hard-working Board of Directors, as well as Daniella, PJ and Joey. Finally, thank you Peter for generously donating the proceeds from this book to our charity.

In addition to the Charity of Hope, Mercanti Management Inc. donates 10% of net profits to The Joy and Hope of Haiti, as well as other charities. If you have travelled to Haiti, as I have, you would understand the need to give.

From its beginning – a group of handball teammates donating five dollars for a young Polish immigrant – Charity of Hope has grown and spread beyond Hamilton to include chapters in Brantford and Oakville, raising over $2 million for our young ones. None of this would be possible without our wonderful sponsors and the generosity of so many people.

Thank you to all of you and God Bless.

Sam Mercanti
Founder and President

My mother and I

QR Code for Charity of Hope

FOREWORD

I have had the pleasure of knowing Peter and his family for many years, and it is an honour to write the foreword to his book. Peter offers his readers great business and leadership tips and the ingredients for a happy life, including the importance of living your life in a manner both honouring and pleasing to the Lord. It's a joy and a treat to read a book that is a wonderful guide for young entrepreneurs, and at the same time, has faith and God at the centre of it all. Peter makes it clear that in one's pursuit of success, God must remain at the centre of it all.

In addition to what Peter offers regarding living a full life, on a philosophical and theological level, the book has scattered throughout it funny and compelling stories. To read the stories about the weddings as well as the many fundraisers, hosting celebrities and stars from around the world, is entertaining and captivating.

Peter has lived a full life; pursuing his dream of business success, meeting celebrities and stars from around the world, fearlessly pursuing his many business interests, treasuring his friendships, raising a wonderful family and most importantly, taking an honest look at his own life.

This book will serve as a teaching lesson for you on many levels. I have found Peter's personal journey especially compelling. He has shared with us his failings and mistakes as well as his successes. He goes further when he confronts his own weaknesses and frailties followed by his own enlightenment. It isn't easy for any of us to reveal the whole story, and even more difficult for anyone to make the difficult pilgrimage within. Through his search, Peter discovers that it is all about God, on a business and personal level. He reveals that life is about following Jesus: forgiving and loving others and ourselves and – most of all – deepening our relationship with the Lord.

I am in many cases best known for scoring some goals in the first Canada Russia Summit Series in 1972, but I would definitely liked to be remembered as a man that followed Jesus and was an encouragement to others. I hope that you are inspired by my friend Peter and his authentic and timely advice that he offers in this book.

Paul Henderson

Paul Henderson

INTRODUCTION

While my event and catering business "Carmen's" was doing the catering for the Hamilton Convention Centre, one of our offices was downtown, right in the heart of Hamilton. We had large picture windows facing Main Street. A homeless man often positioned himself in front of our windows, next to the entrance to our office. My staff complained to me because this man often interfered with customers entering the office. He also impeded our wonderful view of the hustle and bustle of King Street. I eventually approached the homeless man and gave him an offer he couldn't refuse. I offered him twenty dollars if he would go down the street and position himself in front of a luxury hotel owned by a colleague of mine. He agreed, grabbed the twenty and left.

A couple of days passed before he returned and positioned himself, once again, in front of our window by the front door. Frustrated, I approached him and asked why he had violated the deal we made. He informed me that my colleague offered him fifty dollars to return to my place and stand in front of my window. I was willing to negotiate, and he quickly accepted my offer of a hundred dollars to return to the hotel. Sure enough, within a few days he returned to my place informing me that I got outbid once again. I was frustrated, but my pride would not allow me to give up. I negotiated a new deal with him, giving him two hundred dollars if he agreed to alternate his visits every week for a week at each location.

I made the best of the situation by taking every opportunity to go outside and talk with this homeless man whenever it was his week at our location. I discovered that he was a very smart and at one time, a successful businessman. I shouldn't have been surprised given the amount of money he negotiated out of my wallet and the wallet of my colleague. However, difficult times and a couple bad mistakes landed him on the streets.

This experience taught me a lot. First, like the old saying goes, you can never judge a book by its cover. On the outside we all have an appearance, but it's what is on the inside that matters. Secondly, that no matter who you are or what your situation in life, you are somebody; you are important, and you have something to offer the world. Thirdly, good listening skills and valuing what everyone has to offer is a worthwhile endeavour.

I applied these lessons throughout my life in how I conducted my business and personal life. I found this philosophy very effective in applying my leadership skills, developing my business model, and pursuing my own happiness. I offer all of these here for you. If you are a young entrepreneur, I believe my tips and formula for business success and leadership may be of some help to you. If you are someone who is in search of personal fulfillment, wanting to live a spiritual life through redemption and love, I believe this book may be of some help to you also. Or, if you are someone who is just in search of funny stories and would like a peek into the lives of the rich and famous, this book is for you too.

Enjoy!
Peter M.

I have walked in the storming cold rain and
calm warming breeze,
Challenged on every level.
I have experienced success and failure,
The joy of achieving and the pain of sin,
And am grateful for it all.
I have been strong and weak,
walked tall and brought to my knees,
All of it playing its part in making me a better man;
Closer to God, making me more kind, forgiving and friendly.
Because of God and the love of family and friends
I am happy and blessed!

Peter Mercanti

Chapter One

ITALIANS ARE PRETTY SMART

*"Never underestimate anyone,
no matter where they come from or their age." P.M.*

We immigrated to Canada in 1956. I was seven years old. My older brother Sam was nine, and my younger brother Morris was four. Our baby sister Rose would not be born for another four years. My family's first home in Canada was on Picton Street in the north end of Hamilton. From there, it was a second-floor apartment on Catharine Street. Everything was so different from the world we knew: the culture, language, schools, friends. But two constants in our lives helped bind us together and make us strong individuals – the sanctity of family and my mother's lasagna. For Italians, not only is food a significant source of nutrition (fuel to keep us working hard), it brings profound comfort as well. Mealtime is that sacred time of day that would bring us together as a family, sitting around the kitchen table sharing stories and laughter, discussing challenges, and expressing support and love for each other.

Is there any food that smells as good or tastes as delicious as lasagna? It's magical mixture of its assortment of cheeses, meats and tomato sauces with all the added spices. The smell quickly makes its way through your air paths and stimulates every nerve in your brain.

And then, in an instant, your stomach growls, craving that first sumptuous bite. You can taste that first bite long before you take it. It was that wonderful aroma that I remember growing up in Italy as well as here in Canada. Lasagna has followed me throughout my life on both a personal and business level. I hope that you find the material in this book as delicious, as comforting and as nourishing as I have found my mother's lasagna.

When I was eleven years old, we moved to a home at Cannon and Caroline streets. Close by was Wilcox Playground. It was there that I learned to play all sorts of sports – and how to fight so that I could protect myself. I actually turned out to be quite the scrapper, defending my Italian heritage and staking my place in this new land. The Warren family, consisting of a few brothers and a sister, were boxers and also hung out at Wilcox. One day I got into a disagreement with the sister, Brenda Warren. She insisted we settle our dispute with our fists. Confident I would win, I soon discovered she was a better boxer than her brothers. After taking a humiliating beating from Brenda, my brother Sam stepped in to defend me, warning her to never lay a hand on me again. Brenda then beat up Sam as well.

In the 1960's, most Italians who came to Hamilton ended up settling in the North End. It was considered the toughest part of the city. It was mandatory that you learned to fight to survive. It also demanded that we Italians hustle, work hard and be smart if we wanted to make something of our lives. The defeat by Brenda Warren was a crushing blow to my ego. Given my pride and competitive spirit, it set me on an intense search for success and some sort of victory.

Besides playing sports and learning how to fight, Wilcox Playground also offered me an opportunity to make some money.

My brothers and I were always chasing the buck, and the nearby scrap yard, owned by a Jewish family, presented what my friend Sam Macaluso and I considered a golden opportunity. We could make a few dollars and, more importantly, compensate for my defeat at the hands of Brenda. Sam and I watched the scrapyard forklift pile abandoned car engines on top of each other, as it happens, right next to the fence. Sam, being mechanically gifted, even at this young age, made a winch that would pull the engines down off the pile. I would climb the fence, make my way to the top of the engine pile, wrap straps around the top engine and then Sam would pull the engine down using his wench. We would retrieve three engines at a time and pile them on a buggy Sam had also built. The following day, we would return to the scrap yard and sell the scrap engines back to the owner. Three engines earned us one dollar. At that rate, there is no question the scrap yard owners were taking advantage of our youth, but we were willing to settle for fifty cents each on three engines.

We would return to the park on the other side of the fence and watch them pile those same engines back in the same spot we stole them from. We would then wait anxiously for the evening to come in order to steal the very same engines and then sell them back again the next day. Our shrewd and daring victories were exactly what I needed to compensate for the humiliation I suffered at the fists of Brenda Warren.

Years later, I joined the Beverly Golf and Country Club after Carmen's Banquet Centre had been contracted to provide food and beverage services for the Club. The membership of this club was mainly Jewish. I was one of the few Italians to join. One day, a group of us sat around having a great time talking and laughing. One of the Jewish members asked, "Peter, who are better businessmen, the

Italians or the Jews?" I shared with them the story of Sam and I retrieving their engines and then selling them back to them over and over again. I'm not sure if this story convinced them that Italians were better businessmen but I am sure it conveyed the message: "Don't mess with us Italians, especially the ones who are eleven years old." They laughed, appreciating the humour of this story. I always respected my Jewish colleagues, as both our cultures focus on hard work, family, values and faith.

But I'm getting ahead of myself here. Let's start at the beginning. I hope you enjoy walking my journey with me.

Chapter Two

STREETS PAVED IN GOLD

"The weight of poverty is made light when there is love and lasagna." P.M.

Italy

My father, Giuseppe Mercanti, and my mother, Iolanda Mancini, were born and raised in the region of Abruzzo. After an eight-month engagement, they were married on September 14, 1946. Prior to getting married, my father was conscripted into the army and assigned to guard an area in Abruzzo. The army was not well organized, and the soldiers were often near starvation. When the Americans arrived, the Italians were quick to surrender. The Americans sent the Italian soldiers to Algeria as prisoners of war. My father served for three years as a prisoner of war. There they were treated with dignity and were well fed.

While in Italy, my beloved parents had three sons: Sam, myself and Morris. As sharecroppers, my parents had been given a plot of land to work and had to pay a percentage of their profits back to the landowner. They had kept cows, pigs, chickens and rabbits. They also grew their own food, which made our family self-sufficient. We watched both our parents working extremely hard and watched how well they managed what little money they made.

Although we were very poor in Italy, we were rich in family life. We never missed a meal, our clothes were always presentable and we loved and respected each other. When you are rich in family, as a child, you don't realize just how poor you are. We made all our own food, often using our animals as the food source. For instance, chickens provided eggs or could be used for a delicious soup.

My mother had the greatest influence on us, both in those early years and throughout our lives. She was wise – a philosopher, really; the glue that kept the family strong and the captain always steering the ship in the right direction. She was also the money manager, knowing how to stretch every dollar. My father was a simpler person; he was intent on working hard, loving us completely and providing for us as comfortable a life as he possibly could. To him, his job was clear: go to work to make money to provide for his family. There is nothing more noble than working hard so that you can put food on the table for your family.

My mom: kind, loving and financially prudent

Although Italy was turning a corner, there was no future for us there. Our parents just could not see opportunities for a good life for their children in Italy. As for us children, our lives seemed positively wonderful. We played outside, kicked cans like they were soccer balls, chased after chickens and basked in the warmth of our family's unity and love. We were happy in our meagre surroundings. However, our parents wanted something better for us.

My mother would often write to Eugenio, my father's uncle , and ask him what life was like in Hamilton, Canada. Eugenio would write back, "Come to Canada. It is a land of great opportunity and the streets are paved with gold if you want to work hard."

It was unthinkable to us to ever challenge our parents, so when they said we were going to make the long trip to this new land, we had no choice but to cooperate. Not only did we have complete trust in our parents, they were our mentors and, in our hearts, our cherished heroes. My mother's sister's husband, Gino, lent my parents the money for the voyage to Canada. We set sail from Napoli on March 21, 1956 aboard the *Vulcania*.

Boat Ride

Because Mom and Dad had very little money, we occupied the lowest class accommodations on the boat. We were in a part of the ship that reeked of animal waste. Everyone, except myself, got seasick. Throughout the twelve-day trip in April of 1956, as sick as they were, Mom and Dad never showed weakness. Like they did throughout their lives, when they faced tough times, they became tougher.

Our parents were always our rock, our source of love and our very foundation. But it wasn't all love and warm hugs. Mom never hesitated to use the broom on us when we stepped out of line. Dad's preferred method of discipline was to have us get on our knees with our faces up against the wall and hands clasped behind our back. If we held steady, we could avoid the belt.

Like many Italian parents, my parents believed in tough love. Discipline was carried out as part of their love for us. Corporal punishment was not a sign that they did not respect their children. On the contrary, it was done so that we children would be successful in life and avoid bad choices that would bring us suffering. If we ran out onto the road without looking, we would get a whack on the rear end; it was better to get the whack on the rear end than to be hit by a car.

Canada

In April of 1956, we arrived at Pier 52 in Halifax. Our last name was Mercante, but when immigration registered us, they wrote it as Mercanti, the way it sounded. From Halifax, we took a train all the way to Hamilton. For us, arriving in Hamilton would be what it would be like for a child today arriving in Disneyland. It was as if we had travelled to a different world. We saw a city, an actual city, with paved roads and streetlights and rows of buildings and houses. The streets were filled with cars – big and small, beautiful-looking, moving machines. The humble house on Picton Street that my parents rented from my father's uncle appeared grand to us as it had actual rooms, beds to sleep in and a kitchen table.

There are so many characteristics that make Hamilton such a great city. It is beautifully located, surrounded by water with greenery scattered throughout, highlighting wonderful waterfalls and walking trails. Because of the jobs Hamilton offered, it became a place for Italians and many Western Europeans to which to immigrate. It held the promise of living a good life and a bright future. With 60% of Canada's steel produced in Hamilton, the city became the Steel Capital of Canada. Over the past few years, the city has been transformed into an economy based on service and health care. The grit of hard-working people gave rise to the perfect names for this great city: The Hammer, Steeltown and The Ambitious City.

We were in a whole new world. None of us spoke English. I have to admit, we stuck together like scared kittens. Our cousins and uncles kept a close eye on us. We decided that if we stuck together as brothers and with fellow Italians, we had strength in numbers and could make a go of it. We were convinced that we had arrived in the land of opportunity, complete with roads paved with gold. With hard work and hustle, we believed we would succeed. Little did we know the extent of the hard work and struggles we would face to make a go of it in this great new land.

Dad worked in construction but didn't like it. He went on to work for his cousins, Ralph and Frank Mercanti, who owned a number of auto body shops. They gave my father a job at one of them, the West End Auto Body Shop. I looked up to my cousins. In my eyes, they had "made it" and were a success.

Hamilton was surrounded by farms and many Italian immigrants worked on these farms. The farmers would come into the city with their small old bus or trucks and pick up workers at specified locations to take them to their farms. We watched our mother get up very early to work on these farms, her day beginning at 4:00 a.m. At the end of the week, my parents would pool their earnings together on the table and then divide everything into little bundles for items like groceries, shoes, perhaps a wedding gift and, if they were lucky, six dollars to set aside in savings. Not long after arriving, my father sponsored his sister and four brothers to come over.

We eventually moved from the apartment and bought our own house on Cannon and Caroline. We lived on the first floor, my parents renting out the second floor for income. On the third floor, the attic, Sam, Morris and I slept in one bed. That attic also housed my uncles Carmen, Tony and Gabriel. The attic was small with its unfinished peak rafters and barren floor. You had to be careful not to bump your head or get a sliver walking on the wooden floors. It was hotter than hell in that attic, creating an uncomfortable space for sleeping that was conducive to trapping the most foul of smells.

The bed that housed Sam, Morris and I was small, making it almost impossible to find a comfortable spot to sleep. My uncles each had their own small bed. They would return from work at all hours, waking us up walking up the squeaky stairs or making a commotion getting settled in their bed. One of our uncles used a cologne that was so strong, just the smell of it could wake you from a dead sleep. We didn't have the nerve or the heart to tell him about it. Worst than my uncle's cologne was Morris' farts. Not only did they send an unbearable smell throughout the sweltering attic, he would release them like a symphony of song that would wake the mice in the walls. Our escape from these living conditions was close by, as Sam kept our money saved in a box behind a secret compartment in the wall.

Four years after settling in Canada, along came a wonderful miracle, our little sister, Rosanna. Could life get any better than this? No matter the conditions or how few our belongings, to me, Canada was the land of opportunity, and I quickly came to love our city. But little did I know just how much Hamilton would come to mean to me as I grew determined to be an important part of its development, doing my part to contribute what I could.

Chapter Three

THE EARLY YEARS

*"Work hard, fight for what you believe in
and never disappoint your parents." P.M.*

Elementary School

Around the age of ten and for some years following, my father put
my brother Sam and I to work at the body shop. We enjoyed it,
making fifty cents an hour. But my life as an entrepreneur wouldn't
begin until I was eleven. Someone told me that there was money
to be made selling newspapers in downtown Hamilton. We would
buy papers for two cents and sell them for a nickel. This process of
buying something and selling it for more really appealed to me. In
addition to the money I was making, I was motivated by the downtown sights, especially the fancy cars and the people wearing fancy
coats and suits. I admired their success and would say to myself, "If
they can do it, I can do it, too." It fed my competitive spirit but I was
never jealous of anyone. I was only competitive, believing there was
nothing I couldn't do with the gift of the mind God had given me.

Sam and I were selling papers at King and Catharine streets.
Once we exhausted that corner, we would make our way deeper into
the downtown core towards James Street. Each corner had its own
seller, and we would rush to get to a corner before the proprietor
of that corner arrived. This sometimes led to confrontations with

other sellers. They would yell, "Get the f--k off our corner, you dumb Wops!" They would often provoke us to fight because of our heritage. Morris eventually joined us in this business venture, and when we were challenged to fight these vendors, the three of us would lay a beating on them. We quickly learned how to use our fists to muscle our way forward, from corner to corner, and to defend ourselves when others tried to push us around.

We found many ways to make money and quickly realized that the harder we worked, the more money we could make. My brothers and I occasionally worked with my mother on the farm picking strawberries. We also worked at Zellen's Motors, making five dollars for every car we rustproofed. We would spray as many as fifteen cars a day, making what we considered a small fortune. Sam would always save our earnings, keeping it in a safe he had built in woodworking class. Spending all our time working and hanging out downtown taught us to be tough as well as astute. Our circle of friends grew to some forty eager Italians, all sticking together to support and protect one another.

After we sold our newspapers for the day, we would often visit the Farmers' Market and use some of our profits to buy fresh-cut flowers. We would negotiate with the vendors, getting the best price we could – sometimes paying as little as twenty-five cents a bunch. I would take my flowers and visit the nearby hotels, entering through the ladies and escorts entrance. Whenever I saw a lady and her date at a table, with the man's money visible on the table, I would approach the woman and ask her if she would like some flowers. She would smile at me and then tell her companion to buy her some flowers. If he hesitated, the woman would always say: "Give the kid a dollar and buy me some flowers!" It worked. We would double, triple and sometimes earn as much as five times our newspaper money. Our father was making fifty dollars a week, and we were making sixty, all while going to school. Dad thought we were stealing. He was comforted when he eventually realized that we were making our money legitimately and was proud to know that he had instilled in each of us his work ethic.

My brothers and I had by now forged an unbreakable bond. By the time I was twelve, we could smell success. We were confident that we had a lot to offer and that, in this country, the roads really were paved with gold.

Our path to business success was almost interrupted by the priests and nuns who educated us. They tried to convince me, as early as grade eight, to go into the seminary. After all, I had more stars on my board for church attendance than any other student. I was also considered quite bright, despite being a regular recipient of the strap for being overly rambunctious.

I fell in love with all my Italian friends and the bond we formed. We would stick together because non-Italians always wanted to beat us up. The nuns could not persuade me to leave my friends, the exciting life I was living and the possibility of future business success. The foundation for entrepreneurship was laid. Then there was my love for sports, especially after winning the city champion-ship in soccer at St. Mary's elementary school. And, of course, there was the girl factor. I just couldn't do it. I couldn't leave this exciting world to enter the seminary in grade nine.

1961. Hamilton's St. Mary's elementary school soccer champions

1962. Kemp Construction. Pee Wee Police Minor Ontario Baseball Champions

High School

By the time I entered high school, I had developed a passion for sports, for all sports. I had embraced soccer, baseball, hockey, boxing, wrestling, arm-wrestling, football and street fighting. I and my friends who participated in sports were in tip-top shape and tough as nails. My devotion to sports demonstrated my competitive nature and the "I-can-do-it" conviction I brought to all aspects of my life. Whenever I saw someone with nice things or who had experienced success, I would say to myself, "I can do it!"

I was growing every day – in knowledge, in the number of friends I counted, in my interests – but not in height. Some people who are not that tall grow up with a chip on their shoulder. You can't blame them for that because it does have an impact on your athletic abilities as well as on your social life. I actually stopped going to concerts because I couldn't see over the crowd to watch the band. Because of my height, many people felt safe calling me names. They would call me "DP," "wop," "shorty," "grease ball," "spaghetti bender" and "dago." Being Italian certainly caused some of this, but being short played a major part, too.

I have to admit, I did develop a bit of a chip on my shoulder over my height. However, being shorter can also be a blessing. I would tell myself, "God made me this way, and He is proud of me, so I should be proud of myself. What's good for God is good for me." It also lent an edge to my already competitive spirit, making me that much more determined to succeed in all aspects of my life. It even made me a good fighter, developing the attitude that if I couldn't shut them up, I would beat them up. It helped me develop my own technique of fighting that led to the nickname "One-Punch Pete" because I could knock a guy out with one punch. When you are short and can beat up guys twice your size, you feel like you are the king of the world. Perhaps David felt this way after his encounter with Goliath. I would also feel that way when I beat muscle men and "strong men" at arm wrestling. Like the song says, "Ohhhh, what a feeling, what a rush!"

My father was not keen on me playing sports but I never held that against him. A lot of Italian parents back then did not want their kids to play sports. They feared that an injury would impede one's education and work prospects. I would often have team members or coaches pick me up a block away from home so that my father didn't know I was off to play some sport or other.

I had to keep everything related to sports hidden. I kept the athletic crests and medals concealed in a shoebox in the basement. I had roughly thirty to forty crests. One day, my father was cleaning out the basement, found the crests and threw them in the garbage.

I was the pitcher for my hardball team that competed in the CANUSA games. The father of a teammate had taught me how to pitch. I would practise my pitching, putting a basket against the wall of a barn in an open field. I pitched a winning game against Flint, Michigan, striking out twenty-two batters. After winning that game, all the parents were fussing over me, giving me all kinds of accolades. Despite the attention, I remember feeling hollow inside because I wasn't able to share these accomplishments with my parents. On another occasion, unbeknownst to my father, I had spent a weekend playing in a baseball tournament. Upon returning home, I received a tongue lashing from my father for not getting the fence painted. I remember saying to myself, "What's with Italians wanting their fences and railings painted five times? They end up with so many coats of paint it looks like hell."

Many of the Italians went to Cathedral High School. It was the only Catholic high school in Hamilton at the time. Catholic high schools were not fully funded by the province then, so they did not have the facilities, resources or equipment the public schools offered. There was a brand new public high school in Hamilton called Scott Park, which had loads of resources – it even had elevators. Thankfully, my parents let me choose the high school I would attend, and I chose Scott Park. It turned out to be a great choice because of the wonderful new friends I made and the great experiences I had. Around the same time, my parents bought their first house, on Caroline and Cannon streets. It was still in the North End, but it was better than where we had been living, and it became our home.

I continued to play lots of sports through the Catholic Youth Organization as well as in school, playing running back for the junior and senior football teams. I had a strong desire to excel in every sport, even in street fighting. I lived up to my moniker "One-Punch Pete", when I would have to deal with someone who started a fight with me. One time in Buffalo, I was attacked by a guy and I knocked him out with one punch. On another occasion, as an adult, I was attacked by three teenagers but managed to put them all to the ground within a couple of minutes. I have to say, these are moments I am not proud of, even if my actions were justified.

I made a lot of new friends at Scott Park, including my long-time friend, Gabe Macaluso. I acted in the play *Little Abner* and followed that with starting a band with Tony Scutela that we called Indigo. It was a colour I liked, but I also thought it was a cool name. It was the 1960's, the era of great music with the British invasion and the Beatles. It seemed as if everyone was into music. I wanted to be a part of it, and I knew I had a good voice. The members of the band were: Frank Calabrese (organist), Mike Kondershov (our original organist), Pino Garlisi (vocals), Joe Pollici (base), Tony Scutella (band leader, writer, lead and rhythm guitarist), Billy Dika (drummer) and me on vocals. We also had our own booking agent.

My father didn't like the idea of me playing in a band. Like sports, he thought it was a waste of time. However, when he started to see how much money we were making, he had a change of heart. Between the band, the paper route and other sources of income, Morris, Sam and I had a good stash of cash.

One cold winter morning, we saw our mother on her knees polishing the floors. It troubled us to see our mother struggling with this job, so we used the money we had made to buy her a floor polisher from Eaton's department store. We never wanted to see her on her knees again.

It was around this time that I would meet my future wife, Gabriella Fernetti. My best friend Gabe Macaluso and I took the bus to school every day. It was on one of those bus rides that I saw a girl who completely captivated me. I saw her sitting with a folder on her lap with "Gaby" written on it. I think it may have been love at first sight. I was so attracted to her that I just had to pursue her.

It wasn't long before the band was good enough to play Friday night dances in church halls. We often played at All Souls Church hall and, most importantly, Gaby was often there watching us play. We got so good that we started to get paid – and paid well. We were playing festivals and other occasions, and our popularity grew along with our profits. After paying our manager and roadies, we still made a good chunk of change. We would often reward ourselves with Chinese food at a local restaurant after a gig.

We played a lot of originals, ten of which I penned. When I look back, I can see the two sides of myself. There was the lover, expressed in a song I wrote called "I Love You, Yes I Do." I wrote it for Gaby. Knowing that Gaby was going to attend a dance we were performing at, I sang that song to her, introducing the song as being "written for someone very special and you know who you are." And then there is the rebel side of me that I expressed in a protest song I called "Why, Why Why." I was not happy with the Vietnam War, as well as being very disturbed by the assassination of leaders like John F. Kennedy and later, Martin Luther King. This song was played on Hamilton airwaves.

1967. Our band Indigo backs up Roy Orbison

We became fairly popular, getting gigs farther and farther away, and were paid more and more money. In 1967, we were making as much as $1,200 a night. We backed up acts like Roy Orbison, David Clayton Thomas, Anne Murray and Burton Cummings. A music agent approached us a few times and wanted to represent us, talking about putting us on tour from Vancouver to Halifax.

We had a meeting and all of us agreed that the time had come to wrap it up and go our separate directions to make something of our lives. I still remember that emotional meeting we had in the restaurant and us all agreeing that it was time to end the group. It was a difficult decision given our success. Yet there were many reasons that caused us to arrive at this decision, chief among them that our Italian parents would never agree to us going on tour and our love and respect for them was infinite. Plus, some of the guys wanted to go to university. Meanwhile, I was in love with Gaby and wanted to get out into the world to make a life for us. And I'll admit that, as much as I was an extrovert who loved to socialize, I wasn't fond of the world of music with its drugs and chaos. It was a lifestyle that did not appeal to me. However, I do occasionally reflect on how my life would have been different had we had gone on that tour.

In those days, universities would come to high schools to make a pitch for us to attend. I was a good student and I loved to learn, but I had no interest in continuing formal education. The irony of it is that some of my friends who hated school and didn't do all that well continued on to university, entering many careers. Many Italian students, especially those who had come from Italy, quit school early. They had to deal with the language barrier, and many of them had never attended school in Italy. When you added to that parents encouraging them to work, many of them dropped out halfway through high school.

I attended Grade thirteen at Cathedral High School. I knew all the guys there, most of them being Italians from the North End. Despite having good grades, I decided to drop out halfway through the year in favour of getting to work and making money. My brother Sam also dropped out of high school to work at Mercanti Brothers Refinishing. If you had a good attitude and work ethic and were creative and willing to self-educate to become a great entrepreneur, you could become self-sufficient and make good money. I always encourage our young people to take the path they feel called to, whether it is university, the trades or starting one's own business.

I had great teachers at Scott Park, but there were three of them to which I was especially grateful. Al Kingston, my football coach, taught me to be gritty and tough. Bill Powell, who started the Festival of Friends (an annual event that attracts thousands of spectators for an outdoor weekend of entertainment, vendors and foods from around the world), was an easy-going, very nice man who was approachable and helpful. And finally, my electrical teacher, Al Streker, who exercised great patience and always spent extra time explaining anything which with I was having difficulty.

Chapter Four

THE MAN WITH A GUN

"All the money in the world cannot bring any comfort
if acquired the wrong way." P.M.

When you grow up in an Italian home, there are some fundamental factors that are universal. First, there is a deep love and respect for your parents. You obey them and never want to disappoint them. Your family is considered the most important part of your life. Second, there is a strong work ethic combined with a strong desire to provide for your future family. I had these values deep within me, and they helped me arrive at the decision to leave high school. I was completely in love with Gaby and wanted to set the way for us together and the children we anticipated having.

I saw the sacrifices my parents made to provide us with a good life. I was the recipient of their infinite love. I was rewarded with a kind, caring mother who was wise and filled with confidence in all her children's abilities. I wanted to be that kind of husband to Gaby and a good father to my children. This was what was most important to me. We all desire happiness and to live a full and rich life. I believed that marriage, children, working hard and providing for them would bring me that full life. As it turns out, I was right. However, along the way, my desires sometimes overrode reason.

When temptation would set in, I made foolish decisions. The devil comes into your life and tells you that you can accomplish all these well-intended dreams and ambitions if you get off Main Street and come down a side street with him.

By 1977, my partner "Gus" (not his real name) and I had built a pretty good business. We weren't making a lot of money but enough to provide well for our families. Our company, Pioneer Meats Ltd., had twelve employees, and we were providing meat for restaurants in Hamilton, Toronto and Chinatown. We were working hard and aspiring to expand with greater success.

Our driver "Mario" (not his real name) approached me one day and asked to borrow $5,000. That was a handsome sum of money in 1977. He promised me he would double the money and pay it back within a couple of weeks. When I pressed him, wanting to know what he was going to do with the money, he told me that he was going to buy marijuana. I was not one to use drugs or deal in that world in any way, but wanting to help Mario make money, my own greed took hold of me.

Ten days later, Mario gave me $10,000, twice what he had borrowed, as promised. I thought to myself, *Holy shit! That's the easiest $5,000 I ever made.* The devil knocked at my door and I answered, again and again and again. I gave Mario $10,000, and he turned it into $20,000, and then $20,000 was turned into $40,000. I thought this "fast money" was going to help me build my business and provide for my family. Plus, I've always had a rebel side to my personality, and this was certainly fulfilling that. Yet, deep down, I knew that this was not me. I justified it by thinking it was only marijuana and that people have a right to marijuana, and it should be legal. But that would be followed by my thinking, *Are you crazy, Peter? You are breaking the law. You are entering a dark world.*

Just as I was about to put an end to this nonsense, Mario asked for $50,000. He promised it would be the last time. This was a staggering amount of money back then. Greed got the best of me again, and I went along with it. At this point, I was concerned about who would be protecting my investment. My money would be delivered in trade to some shady characters, and I wanted to know if Mario was flying solo. When Mario admitted there was only him, I decided to send my friend "Sal" (not his real name) with him. Given Sal's history, I was confident he would protect my investment.

Sal was from Sicily and hung out at the Italo Canadian Club. I enjoyed going to the club where there were Italians like me, grinding it out trying to make a living. It also had a lot of mobsters. I got to know many of them, but I would never do business with them or get involved with them in that way. And yet, I had a lot of respect for them. They never bothered anybody, and I always found them to be perfect gentlemen. That's the way they were in the club; I couldn't speak to what went on outside the club.

To further protect my investment, I decided to follow them to the water crossing at Windsor and watch the transaction from a distance. I remember saying to myself on that drive: P*eter, what the hell are you doing? This is not you. You are a good, honest man. This is not like you. You shouldn't be doing this. It's just not right.* Then I heard another voice say to me, "Peter, this is the easiest money you will ever make. You have been grinding it out and fighting your way up since you were a kid. You deserve this. Just think of how this money will help provide for your family." Saint Peter and the Devil Peter were doing battle.

I parked my car and watched from a distance as the boat pulled up to the shore to meet Mario and Sal. As three large men got out of the boat with a couple hockey bags of marijuana, Sal pulled back his jacket exposing his gun and letting them know he was ready to use it if they tried anything funny. My gut told me that if Sal wasn't there, they would kill Mario and take the money and marijuana. They made the exchange and got back into the boat, and Sal and Mario got into the car. I breathed a sigh of relief, got back in my car and began the drive back to Hamilton. All the way home, the conflicting thoughts continued, tearing me between two worlds. I figured I was in the clear, but when I returned to my factory at 2:00 a.m., all hell broke loose.

Ooops, I'm getting ahead of myself again. Let's go back and I'll explain what happened prior to this big mistake.

Chapter Five

GETTING ON WITH IT

*"Opportunities will come and go,
but the love you give lasts forever."* P.M.

I was head over heels with Gaby and wanted to start my life with her. Gaby was Italian, but when I met her parents, their northern Italian dialect was so different from the Abruzzo dialect, I thought they were speaking a different language. But it didn't matter to me whether she was Italian or not, this was the woman for me. To this day, my favourite song is "My Girl" by the Temptations because it speaks to me of my Gaby.

Gaby and I got married in 1970. In Italy, Abruzzo is known for its wonderful food and hospitable people. Thankfully for me, Gaby was eager to learn how to cook and learned from my mother; I have eaten like a king ever since. It's as if I never left Abruzzo. When I was twenty, we were given our first miracle: a beautiful baby girl we named Daniella. Gaby named her, and I loved the name. It truly is a miracle when a little angel is brought into the world. It is incredibly powerful to walk into the hospital as two people and leave as three. Although ambition and a competitive spirit always was a part of who I was, the blessing of a child as well as the responsibility to provide further motivated me to hustle and provide a good life for my family.

I got my first full-time job in an accounting office at National Steel Car. I was there until I got a better job at F.G. Bradley Meat Company in Toronto. They were a big firm, one of the first companies to make portion-controlled hamburger patties. This was a great opportunity for me to learn about the food business. F.G. Bradley supplied all the best restaurants, the Hilton as well as the airlines. They provided portion-controlled steaks, beef and other meats. They trained me to be a buyer. Given how my career would unfold, this was the perfect start in the world of hospitality.

It was while I was working at this company that I came in contact with a man who would become my mentor, Pat Paletta. Paletta Brothers Meat Products Ltd. provided F.G. Bradley with certain products. Once we met, Pat and I immediately took to each other. In addition to us both being Italian and hitting it off so well on a business and personal level, Pat saw potential in me. He offered me a job with double the salary and the keys to a Ford LTD. I loved my new job. Pat and I got along so well, I was learning a lot from my new mentor and had more money in my pocket to provide for my family. F.G. Bradley taught me about portion control, and Paletta was about to teach me about the livestock industry.

Pat had three demands: 1) be at work by 7:00 a.m.; 2) when required, work six or seven days a week; 3) learn every aspect of the plant. I had a great work ethic and was eager to learn. By 1972, I was learning every step on the slaughter line as well as learning a lot from Pat about what it takes to create a successful business. I studied how he negotiated with other businessmen, how he paid attention to every detail and the steps he would take to build his real-estate empire. I admired his work ethic and his determination to make enough money, as he put it, "to afford his children and grandchildren every opportunity."

Pat admired my work ethic, tenacity, ambition and competitive nature. Pat also appreciated how much money I was making for his company. I approached past clients in Toronto and managed to convince them to return to do business with us. Pat appreciated me winning them back over. Pat also knew how to needle and joke with me. I was expected to arrive every morning at 7:00 a.m. I would always be at work at 6:45. I would walk by his office and say "Hi" to him. He would return the greeting by saying, "Good afternoon." I would return his joking criticism by sometimes showing up at 5:00 a.m. and saying to him when he arrived, "Good afternoon, Pat."

Pat also had his own unique ways of letting me know how grateful he was for my work and talents. In a complimentary way, he would say to me, "You know, Peter, not anyone could be a Frank Sinatra." Pat thought I was special and unique, and this was his way of telling me that I was like Frank Sinatra.

I encouraged Pat to go after the big stores. Pat believed that we could never get into the big stores because they wouldn't be receptive to Italians. As it turns out, I was successful in getting our product into Dominion stores, now Sobey's. I even managed to get my old employer, F.G. Bradley, to buy more products from Paletta.

Pat would often bring me to his high-profile real estate meetings in Toronto. His Toronto partners respected him, often asking him for his opinions. They often called him "The Butcher." I relished every minute, watching and listening to his every word and watching how he would negotiate and work with them to make big business deals.

Pat brought his son Angelo into the company to work in the summers. I was honoured when Angelo's mother asked me to mentor him. Angelo was a great worker and extremely inquisitive, asking me an endless list of questions to learn everything he could. It was great working with Angelo and seeing the great potential in this young teen.

I was and remain forever grateful to Pat Paletta. He came from Italy with nothing and built an empire. To a young guy like me, Pat was an infinite source of knowledge. I studied every move he made and was constantly inspired by him in business but also on a personal level. He was brilliant but also a visionary who could see the trends. It was as if he could see into the future. He had his own formula before there were any self-help books on business. He knew, for example, that real estate would boom some day. So while he was running his meat-packing plant, he was buying up real estate. One method he used was to personally approach old farmers who were ready to retire and offer to buy their farms.

Perhaps God sent Pat into my life at that young age to mentor and guide me. He truly wanted the best for me, sending me to Chicago to earn a certificate in the food industry and paying $100 for me to attend the Dale Carnegie course, "How to Win Friends and Influence People." That course had a major impact on my life.

Despite how hard I was working for Pat, how generous he was to me and the success I was experiencing, I wanted something more. I was like a volcano inside with an infinite amount of energy ready to erupt. With my love for working with numbers, I took a tax course at H&R Block to learn about tax laws and how to do tax returns. After receiving my certificate, I went to Padovani Travel Agency at Barton and James and asked them if they had anyone who did taxes for the Italian immigrants and offered my services. In addition to Padovani providing travel services for the Italian community, they would help the Italian immigrants with all sorts of issues regarding government forms, employment papers and more. Luckily they didn't have anyone to do the tax returns. They were excited at my offer and promised me ten returns the following day.

The tax returns started flooding in, and my small home on Murray Street was no longer sufficient. I rented a space next to the Tivoli on James Street North for $150 a month and put in two desks: one for me and one for the person I would hire. I called my new business "Hamilton Tax Services." I was charging $30 per tax return, paying $5 to Padovani for the referral and clearing $25 a return. I eventually hired a retired gentleman whom I would pay $15 for every return he did. After paying him, I was clearing $10 on every return without having to do anything.

We were doing the taxes for people in all walks of life: farmers, mechanics, labourers and trades people. I always had people sign a disclaimer so that if they did not report something on their taxes, I was not responsible. Some trades and small business people would have me do their returns not claiming the cash they made. It was none of my business what they did. Some would come in with every "i" dotted and every "t" crossed, claiming every penny from cash jobs. It was 1973 and I especially remember one plumber who made $100,000 in a year. *My God*, I thought to myself, *this guy makes more than a lawyer.* If people came in with a disorganized shoebox of receipts, I would charge them an additional $150 to do the book-keeping for the tax return.

Meanwhile, Pat gave me a raise and work with him was becoming so demanding that I couldn't devote time to my tax business. If you can believe it, I began to feel guilty about making so much money for not doing any work in the tax business. Basically, the gentleman I hired was doing it all.

This older gentleman was overwhelmed when I offered him the tax business for free. It made me feel good to do this for him, and I remember feeling overjoyed when I heard he had brought his son into the business. I was so swamped with my work with Pat that I decided I had to completely focus on that work. This older gentleman arrived when I needed him the most, and he did such a wonderful job he deserved the business. I had a desire to do a kind thing – the right thing. It felt good to me to give him the business rather than sell him the business. Hamilton Tax Services remained in business for decades.

Pat brought Gus, a smart, hard-working man, into his company. We quickly became good friends and developed a great deal of trust between us. As much as Gus and I loved Pat and were grateful for the opportunities he offered and for his mentoring, we had an itch to go it on our own. McDonald's built Caravelle Foods in Mississauga, and we provided them with hamburgers. McDonald's asked us to consider buying a franchise. Gus and I applied and were approved for the McDonald's franchise at Upper Gage and Mohawk in Hamilton. I had everything set up and $35,000 ready to purchase the franchise. But when it came down to the crunch, we backed out because McDonald's told us we could not be partners – there could only be one owner.

Shortly after walking away from that, we approached Wendy's. We had the opportunity to own Hamilton's first franchise on Upper James in Hamilton. This time, Gus and I could not agree to the strict rules and guidelines set by Wendy's head office. We moved forward, getting everything done to purchase a Hooter's franchise but backed out at the last minute because we didn't want our wives to leave us.

When I look back, I view these two decisions as financially poor ones. We are well aware that McDonald's and Wendy's took off, becoming very valuable franchises. However, if I had bought one of those franchises it could have changed the entire course of my life. I would have missed out on the exciting years that followed, operating a great banquet hall, sharing in the joy of thousands of brides and grooms and their families and holding special events and meeting celebrities from around the world.

Pat was not happy with our decision to leave and go into business for ourselves. And yet, he was completely supportive knowing that nobody could curb our enthusiasm. Some people said I was crazy to leave my mentor, a good position with a great company, a great salary and a bright future. But I was willing to leave security for insecurity. Such life-altering decisions are risky, but I had to fly on my own. More important than what anyone else thought, my wife Gabriela was completely supportive and never questioned my decisions. In fact, her constant support and faith in me contributed to any success I experienced in my life.

Chapter Six

THE GOOD SAMARITAN
AND THE MOOSE

"Love will come along at the most unexpected times.
Be prepared!" P.M.

G us and I bought a 36-acre farm with a plant on it in Fulton, Ontario. We opened our own company called Pioneer Meats. We paid $40,000 for the farm and invested another $60,000 to convert the 3,000-square-foot existing plant into a meat and beef processing plant. This was a lot of money in the early 1970's. We had saved enough money that we had seventy-five percent cash and took out a loan for the difference.

The farm had an 1,800-foot frontage. It also had a farmhouse that we rented out to a man who paid rent and farmed the land. We would bring in carcasses and debone them into prime rib and tenderloin cuts. We bought a truck and hired a crew to deliver our products. We were doing well, but business wasn't exactly booming. With any new business venture, there is phenomenal stress. Sometimes you feel like you are in the middle of the ocean, alone and unsure if you will make it to land. It's a terrible feeling, especially when you're intent on providing a good life for your family.

I'm sure you've heard the Parable of the Good Samaritan. A Jew is beaten and left in a ditch. People pass him by, including some you would expect to help him. Finally, a Samaritan – often viewed as unfriendly toward Jews – comes along and helps the man in the ditch. I suppose one of the messages Jesus is teaching in this parable is that help can come when you least expect it and from the most unlikely of sources.

A man whom we had never seen before came into our factory and asked us to cut a moose that he had killed. I agreed and we got talking. He worked for the government in Niagara region. I asked him if we could legally sever our 36 acres, separating the house with 30 acres from the plant with six acres. Not only was he confident that we could, he offered to do all the paperwork. He obviously knew what he was doing and had some influence because the region agreed to it. We severed and sold the 30 acres with the house for $40,000 and kept six acres and the plant.

A while later this Good Samaritan returned and told us we could sever the six acres into four lots, keeping one acre with our plant and selling the remaining three. We were elated at the prospect of this opportunity. Once again, he helped us through the process and, after meeting with approval for our plans, we sold each lot for $40,000. All of this was accomplished in two years.

I offered the Good Samaritan some money, but he wouldn't take it. In fact, he wouldn't take anything. He was just a kind man who wanted to help us. The whole experience was rather surreal. It was as if an angel was sent to help us with our new business. To think, a dead moose and a kind man changed our lives.

When I think back to a time in 1976, I'm actually dumbfounded by what transpired next in my life – my first big mistake. I explained what happened back in Chapter Four. I believe I left off with me driving back to my factory at 2:00 a.m. I was met on the road by cars with bright lights coming towards me. Three cars blocked me from entering my factory lot. Two large men got out of their car and approached mine, one of them now standing next to my car and holding a shot gun next to my head. They were plain-clothes police officers, and they ordered me out of the car. Officer Bruce Elwood told me I was being arrested and charged with conspiracy.

Officer Elwood was somewhat sympathetic and told me that I was probably trapped in a situation in which I didn't understand the gravity. He explained how they had our phones tapped because our driver Mario was caught twice before for marijuana. I had no idea that our driver had a history like this, but I certainly knew what was going on. Within two days, the story was plastered all over the local newspaper, followed by police coming to my home and traumatizing my wife. Poor Gaby. She is the perfect wife and as innocent as can be. She didn't deserve this. The shame I brought to her and the family was almost unbearable for me.

I solicited a powerful defence lawyer who gouged me for $25,000 just as a retainer. Now, my $50,000 for the marijuana buy was gone and an additional $25,000 to the lawyer. And I was charged, bringing embarrassment and trouble to the family. What a bloody mess I had got myself into. I posted bail the next day, but my driver remained in jail. I visited Mario in jail and whispered to him, "Where the hell is the marijuana?" The police hadn't found it, and I just wanted my money back. Mario told me the location, and I arranged for a tough guy to retrieve it for me. I made it clear to this tough guy that I did not want to make any money and just wanted my initial investment of $50,000 back. He retrieved the marijuana, and I got my $50,000 back by having it sold at cost.

When it came to the court case, everyone pleaded guilty except Gus and I. I argued that I only loaned Mario the money, and that it had nothing to do with his business dealings. My lawyer was disappointing, and I ended up having to do three months in the slammer, but I was allowed to work during the day. Judge Walter Stayshyn was fair, Officer Elwood spoke on my behalf and Walter Zimmerman encouraged me to apply for a pardon. Zimmerman went to Stayshyn and had him write a letter on my behalf, granting me a pardon. I think the only person who let me down was the one I paid ... my lawyer. Ironically, Stayshyn, Zimmerman, Elwood and I ended up becoming good friends.

I've never taken a drug in my life and never got involved in that world, other than this one mistake. Yet, to this day, people will say to me: "I know how you made your money. You made your fortune with drugs. You are in the mob. You are Italian and everyone who is Italian is crooked." This is what I have had to live with for decades because of this mistake. And, my family has had to tolerate that shame for decades. When I think of it, it makes me ill.

There may have been some good that came from all of this. Good can certainly come from our mistakes if we work at it. Here are three of many important lessons I learned from this mistake:

1. Greed always ends badly. Earn your money the clean way. Grind it out and don't look for short cuts to success. You are truly free when you know you have done it the right way.

2.   You have to learn to shake gossip and lies. It's difficult enough living with regrets and any shame you bring your family, but you can't allow yourself to get entangled in other people's lies and gossip.

3.   If you make a mistake or shake hands with greed, as much as you try to forgive yourself, you will never forget it. You have to live with that. Even more difficult is watching your family having to deal with it. Greed and sin bring too much pain. It can promise you the entire world, but it isn't worth it. The price is just too high.

Chapter Seven

A NEW PATH

*"God gave us a brain with infinite potential.
So get going and use it." P.M.*

Gus and I continued with the business for three more years. We were doing okay, keeping our heads above water. In 1978, Morris, Sam and I invested in Carmen's Bakery to help our Uncle Carmen. The investment bought the property and paid to put up the building. Uncle Carmen only sold bread at first. He knew how to make great bread, but you know what they say, "Man cannot live on bread alone." My brother Morris would say; "There is no dough in making dough."

The bakery wasn't doing as well as we had hoped. We were all too busy to put time into helping Uncle Carmen. I was working on my meat company; Sam was busy with his own body shop, Ontario Auto Collision; and Morris was teaching. While making a delivery to Brantford, Uncle Carmen got into a serious accident and suddenly the bakery had no baker. We scrambled to find a good baker and to keep the store open. We even tried to sell the business and the building but couldn't find buyers. Gus and I decided to separate, him buying me out so that I could work full-time at the bakery.

I came up with a business plan that involved changing the use of the space in the bakery. I started to sell pastries, and I put in freezers to sell frozen steaks as well as a counter to sell cold cuts and cheeses. The business started to do well, setting the trend for a lot of stores to diversify. When Uncle Carmen recovered and returned after a few months, it was a whole new business. When he saw what we had done, he was not happy. It wasn't what he had envisioned. The three of us bought Uncle Carmen's share, and eventually he started the very successful business Sweet Paradise with his sons.

Not long after, Gaby and I attended a wedding. At the reception dinner, out came the bread rolls. I said to myself, "Hey, those are our rolls from the bakery." Then the antipasto trays came out, and again I said to myself, "Hey, that is our meat and cheese from our deli." When the lasagna and later the pastries came out, I repeated the same lines. Attending that wedding was a business changer for me. It pushed me to make up my mind – we would start to cater weddings.

I believe Italians are good at filling the gap. They see a need and they fill it. This business strategy made many of them very successful. Many of them couldn't spell their names, but they became multi-millionaires by filling a gap. It's an interesting study to try to understand why so many Italians have become successful in business. Perhaps it's because they are naturally talented at business or that they are not afraid of risk. It may be because of the love and support they get from family or perhaps an impoverished background really motivates them.

As a person of gratitude, I take this opportunity, once again, to say "thank you" to Uncle Carmen, my other uncles, family, staff and my parents for bringing us to Hamilton and providing the support to facilitate success. We were now catering to weddings in church basements. Some of my first employees included: Carla Sencic, Frank Wilson, Tracey Robinson, Jackie Cooke, Pauline Oulette and Louie DiDometti. Many of them stayed for years to come.

1985. An early Carmen's filling the gap! Morris, myself and a happy staff on the way to business success

I was always competitive. It was my competitive nature that drove me to do all the things I did, even those things that my parents found difficult to agree with. The catering aspect of the business exploded. We eventually started doing "full service", which included decorations and flowers. We were now renting halls throughout the entire area to accommodate the number of weddings and events we were catering.

When I discovered Royal Botanical Gardens, I found out that they were only renting for flower shows. They quickly agreed to my proposal to rent the facility to us to do weddings. They didn't have a kitchen, but we would make the food off-premises and bring it in. I could charge a lot for weddings at the RBG because the setting was beautiful and couples loved the flower gardens. I secured a two-year, exclusive contract with the RBG. Competitors quickly caught on and were jealous. They raised a stink and I had to share the facility with two other caterers.

I was now renting many facilities, including legion halls to host weddings. Cooking off-premises, transporting food, dealing with stairs and other inconveniences started to get quite annoying. In addition, these places started to raise their rental fees at an accelerated pace. In 1982/1983, I was paying $300,000 a year to rent halls. I originally rented St. Gregory's Church Hall for $10,000 a year, being given all open Saturdays. The following year, the priest charged $30,000 and then $60,000 the year after that. Whoever said that priests aren't good businessmen? Rental fees for all these places became so ridiculous that the time had come to make a move – to build or buy our own hall. Not only would we own the property and building, we would save a lot of money on transportation and the now-ridiculous rental fees and save a lot of trouble with the logistics.

We originally planned to build one hall, but doing ten to fifteen weddings per weekend would require several halls. Even several halls weren't enough to satisfy my vision. I didn't want a building that was built like a box. I wanted something beautiful, something brides would fall in love with, a place that would be the talk of the town.

Henry Merling, a powerful alderman in Hamilton, was a big help in making this dream come true. He found the property on Stone Church Road, surrounded by nothing but farmland then. He had a vision of the development that would come to that area with future buildings and expressways. People thought I was crazy to buy in this area, but Henry's vision and my intuition were right. When couples saw the drawings of the hall to be built, the bookings for the following year started to pour in. Their deposits gave us the cash flow we needed.

I started to put together a very detailed and sophisticated business plan. With interest rates at fifteen percent, the banks were laughing at my idea. The idea of having a hall primarily for weddings was a novel idea for the time. I met with many banks, and I would ask the bankers, "Are you married?" They would answer "yes", and I would remind them that almost everyone gets married and that brides want a beautiful place in which to be married. It was a convincing argument. They bought the proposal and were willing to finance our dream. Our bakery on Concession was paid off, and we sold it for $450,000. The cost of the land, hall and banquet centre was $3 million. We financed $2.5 million at a high rate of interest, but the mortgage payments turned out to be only slightly more than what we were paying to rent all those halls.

I hired Nick Di Philps, a young McMaster engineering graduate, to assist in the building of our dream hall. It had to be built and operating in a staggering nine months. Nobody thought it could be done.

We started building Carmen's in March of 1988. To meet all the pre-signed wedding contracts and fulfill my own vision, I had to have this spectacular hall built and ready to go by the end of September of that year. Although interest rates were high at the time, there was still a lot of building happening in the area so it was a challenge to get the right tradespeople for my project. With the spectacular architecture of our building and the number of large, beautiful blocks to be laid, I knew it would be a challenge to find the best tradespeople we needed. Everyone thought my expectation for completion was unreasonable and that I would never meet my goal.

xThe first thing I did was visit sites where major construction was being done. I found the most skilled labourers, especially block- and bricklayers. At one site, with the permission of the site foreman, I approached some highly skilled labourers and offered them a 5-hour evening shift with a $10 raise. It was a lot to ask of workers who had already put in a full day of hard labour. But the raise appealed to them and they took the job.

I wondered if some of the guys would be too tired to work 4 to 9 p.m. so I provided the fuel they needed by having them served a nutritious supper every night. Thinking this might not guarantee a productive shift, I went a step further. I hired a very attractive woman to serve them their food every evening. She dressed and acted perfectly for the part. The men were tickled and productivity went way up. Brick and stone were being laid faster than I had ever seen before!

The evening working and good looking waitress caused quite a commotion in the area. People slowed down and stared when they drove by and I had other workers calling me trying to get on the team. It even drew the attention of the police. When they visited, I had to reassure them that everything was legal and on the up and up. To win their favour, I invited them to join my workers for dinner every evening. They were delighted and, sure enough, they came every evening to be served dinner by this beautiful woman and kept a strict eye on the operation, and mostly the woman, as they ate in their car.

There wasn't a hall like it anywhere. People throughout Canada were impressed, including those who travelled from the USA for weddings and events. I cannot emphasize enough the stress and worry my brothers and I had. But businesspeople are always worried, and it was our confidence and determination that would override our worries and apprehension.

Carmen's took off, with our hall being *the* place to get married. We ended up doing as many as twelve weddings per weekend. It takes a lot of people and a good team to make something work, and I am grateful to all of them.

Chapter Eight

THE MOB AND ME

"If you mind your own business,
you can do business with anyone." P.M.

Contrary to the many rumours that got back to me, I am not a mobster, and I had no dealings with the underworld. One of the great things about writing your own biography is that you can dispel the myths, put an end to false gossip and tell the truth. I have heard several of the false stories told about me over the years. One of those rumours was regarding "The Mob." Hamilton is known to be a very active city when it comes to so-called Mob Families. Hamilton has had its share of crime and mob involvement. Because I am Italian and a successful businessman, I have been accused of being associated with those families.

As I explained earlier, Carmen's Bakery took off in the mid-1980's when we diversified. At the time, there had been bakeries that were bombed with new owners conveniently taking over. One of the bakeries that was bombed had a baker who was the best cannoli maker in the city, maybe the best in the world. He was now out of work, and I was eager to bring him to Carmen's Bakery. His cannoli brought us a small fortune in revenue.

I was paid a visit by the son of a local family boss. I was told that his father wanted me to stop making cannoli because they were cutting into that family's business. Angry and stubborn, I told the kid to leave and to go back and tell his father that if he had a message for me, he could come and deliver it himself. Word got out on the street that this family wanted me to stop making my cannoli. At the same time, there was another mob boss in the city who frequently visited the bakery and would buy food from us. When he heard about the problem, he offered to help. I told him sternly, "I'll handle it."

My family was frightened and, I have to admit, I had some fear as well. Yet my conscience would not allow me to concede control to anyone. Time passed and, as I calmed down and reflected, I became fearful that if our bakery was to be bombed, it could kill some of my family members. I spoke to the mob boss who offered to help me. He met with the other family and negotiated a compromise: I had to stop selling wholesale, but I could sell retail out of my store. This compromise would save our store from possibly being bombed, my family from being injured and I knew that no harm would come to our cannoli maker.

Years passed and Carmen's Banquet Centre was hosting thousands of weddings. One day, my secretary came into my office to tell me there was a family that wanted to see me. It turned out to be the same family that had put an end to my wholesale cannoli business. *Oh boy, what now?* I wondered. The father of the family pulled me aside to speak in private. He told me he wanted to have a family wedding at Carmen's. I tried every tactic to convince him that he ought to consider having it at another very well-run banquet hall not far from ours. I told him they had a beautiful hall, the price was cheaper and the down payment was less. He was insistent that his daughter would have her reception at Carmen's. He gave me an offer I couldn't refuse.

He paid the deposit and his daughter's wedding went off wonderfully. We attended to every detail he requested and served them a great meal. The next day, I was called to the father's home. When I arrived, I was greeted as a friend, and we enjoyed a shot of whisky together. I was then handed a large bag of money. When I returned to my office, I asked my secretary to sort and count it. She discovered there was $3,000 more than what had been billed in the bag. I returned to the home with the bag containing the excess $3,000 and told the father he overpaid. The father simply said, "You are an honest man. That is your tip, give it to your staff who did a great job."

Over the years, I did his other children's weddings as well as many other families in Hamilton. I found them to be sincere, forthright people who always kept their word. They were always respectful, very well behaved and disciplined. When dealing with them from the business end, they were perfect gentlemen. Their weddings were always large events, having as many as 700 guests. They always paid in time and in full. They never abused the hall, always leaving it in great shape. What these people do in their own life is their business. I respected that.

Oh, I forgot to mention something. I had a friend come to me whose brother was in trouble with one of these families. His brother owed a lot of money. My friend asked if I would help by negotiating something with the mob family in question, suggesting a payment plan. His brother owed more money than he could ever repay unless he was put on some kind of payment plan without interest accruing. Fearing for my friend's brother's life, I agreed to try to help.

I met with the boss of the family. He, along with others in this family, was happy to see me and greeted me with open arms. At that point, I knew I had a chance. I explained the situation and asked if something could be worked out. He asked me to step outside, allowing him to have a private meeting with his crew. They had a five-minute meeting and then came out to get me. They told me I could convey to my friend that the $100,000 debt was forgiven. I have to admit, I was shocked by their generous offer and understanding of the situation.

Let me make it clear that, aside from this incident and hosting all their weddings and events, I was never involved in their business ventures nor did I do any business with them. There may be rumours out there to the contrary, but I speak the truth. Italians in general, especially those successful in business, get a bad rap. It's assumed that we are all in the mob or connected in some way. Believe me, we are smart enough to make millions the legal way.

Chapter Nine

MY LIFE AT CARMEN'S BANQUET HALL

"I have always worked hard and dreamed big,
that has been the secret of my success." P.M.

It was 1987, and our vision had come to fruition. Sam, Morris and I had one of the most beautiful banquet halls in the country. I was grateful to architect John Romanov and to Nick Di Philps, who helped me do all the sub-contracting and to oversee the building of the hall. When you avoid hiring a builder, as we did, you save some fifteen percent of the total cost. Also, you hold total oversight of the project. As I previously mentioned, weddings would normally be hosted in small halls, legions and church halls. My brothers wanted to build one hall, but I was insistent on one big hall that could be divided into three sections to accommodate three weddings at once. It proved to be a wise decision.

We hired a Sicilian chef, who wouldn't allow you to get within five feet of him. He never wanted anyone, not even fellow cooks, to see his secret recipes. We had a staff of eager employees. People were so grateful to have a job and would never push the limits to see what they could get out of us. A great hall, a master chef, hard-working employees and our own hard work would be the perfect ingredients for our success. Successful it was, with everyone wanting to book their wedding at Carmen's. We filled the gap!

In the 1980's and 1990's many weddings, especially Italian weddings, were planned by the parents. Often, the parents of the bride and groom would come to the planning meeting, sometimes with a set of grandparents. Times have changed, and today it's the bride and groom making the plans.

I reserved Saturdays from 10:00 a.m. to 3:00 p.m. to meet personally with potential customers. I loved the whole process involved in selling. I had my own method to selling. When potential clients come in to talk to me, I knew that they had probably visited other halls. Making the sale was a high and fed my competitive spirit. I really enjoyed meeting people, especially the bride and groom. Meeting the parents of the bride and groom was also enjoyable. I wanted to get to know them beyond the planning of the wedding booking. I would ask them questions about their life and how they met.

Every interaction and sale presented a whole new host of experiences. How people met and the lives they lived fascinated me. At one time, only parents came to arrange the wedding. They viewed it that because they were paying they would make the arrangements. They almost always wanted to communicate with me in Italian. I like that because it kept my Italian sharp. When the bride and groom attended the meetings, they would make it clear to their parents that they wanted to communicate in English.

You never knew who was going to come through those doors to discuss their wedding. One customer was a middle-aged Italian couple arranging their daughter's wedding. The husband was as quiet as a mouse, and it was obvious that he feared his wife. He never spoke a word, leaving all the talking and planning to her. She went on and on, in her thick Italian accent, about how she wanted every detail covered, including what was to be on the menu. After she finished talking, her husband sheepishly requested, in his thick Italian accent: "Okay, you finishe?"

"Yeah," she replied, "I'm a I finishe. Why?"

"You speka," he told her, "now I a speaka."

He explained how he did not like her choices for the menu; one of his complaints being that the pasta she chose would make a mess on everyone's dress clothes. He also had a problem with the anti-pasto she had ordered.

As soon as he finished talking, his wife jumped up, went around the table to where he was sitting, stuck three fingers in his face and said, "Let me tella you a sometin. You only have a three things to do with da wedding. You show upa, shut upa and paya upa."

Before it turned into a full-blown war, I jumped in and was able to calm them down and offer some suggestions regarding the menu. They simply responded, "Okaya, Peter, we trusta you." It was a happy ending to a rocky start.

In many cases, the women wore the pants in the family and decided on the details of the wedding. Sometimes parents came from different regions of Italy. They would get into serious discussions, sometimes arguments, regarding the food they wanted served. They wanted to cater to their friends and family, and each was convinced that the food from their region was better. I would try to cool down the arguments by offering a variety of food, representing the regions they were from.

There were situations where the bride and groom would come to a meeting, and I would find myself rather surprised, sometimes shocked, when I met them. One of them would be drop-dead gorgeous/handsome with a body to die for and the other would be ... the opposite. My insatiable curiosity would get the best of me and I would ask nicely, "You seem to be a mismatch. How do I have this honour to meet you, and how did you get to this stage in your life?" Surprisingly, they knew what I was getting at but were never offended. They would explain to me that they were attracted to the other's kindness or sense of humour or their personality. Some of you reading this may consider my forwardness to be pushy or presumptuous, but I just couldn't help myself. Just another one of my weaknesses.

At one wedding, a bridezilla shared with me that she spent $25,000 on her wedding dress. I bit my lip, and it took everything in me not to say, "You can spend $100,000, and it wouldn't make a damn bit of difference." I have seen brides of simple means look dazzling in their humble wedding dresses.

On another occasion, two tall, handsome Italian twins showed up to book a double wedding. These brothers were identical to the point that you could not tell them apart. They had the exact same body structure, the same face, the same voice and the same tone. They began to tell me what they wanted for their double wedding. At first, I suspected that my brother Morris was playing a trick on me. (We were always playing tricks on each other.) I thought to myself, *Who in their right mind would come to plan a wedding without the bride?*

I stopped them and asked, "Where are the women?" As soon as they began to explain, I stopped them again and said, "I don't want to waste your time, and I don't want you to waste my time. I don't plan a wedding without the bride. Go back home, get your fiancées and then come back." All along, I was convinced that this was a hoax and that Morris was behind it. But Morris vehemently denied there was any hoax. When they called to rebook an appointment with me, I realized it was for real.

They returned with their brides-to-be. I asked them if the brothers were different in any way and could they tell them apart. The women said that the brothers were exactly alike in every single way, from head to toe. (I wasn't sure how they would have known that, but that's a story for another day.) The women explained that the only way they could tell them apart was by their cologne, as each preferred to wear a different scent. I couldn't help but think of the trouble it could cause if the twins were to switch colognes.

One bride was Scottish and the other one was Greek, so it turned out to be one of the most fascinating weddings I have ever seen. The Scottish, Greek and Italian cultures were mixed together to include traditions, music and foods from each. We managed to accommodate all three traditions every way they wished. The reception was beautiful and was one heck of a spectacle. I found the mixture of music fascinating, and I was shocked to see the floor covered in money when the people danced with the Greek bride. Years later, the movie *My Big Fat Greek Wedding* was released. It reminded me in some ways of the wedding at Carmen's.

I believe I was always a good salesman, but there were people who would really get under my skin. Some people were so cheap they would nickel and dime me on every single item, right down to a flower bud. I would get so frustrated that I would tell them if they got the hell out of my office I would give *them* money. The other extreme was those who would spend in excess of $100,000 to have every detail managed. They could be so fanatical, they would practically ask for the floor tiles to be changed.

In the earlier years, weddings were less complicated. We would provide the hall, the food and the decor. With social media, they would compare their plans with what had already been done and would shoot for something new and different. No matter how simple or complex a wedding is, I always say that the foundation remains the same – it all starts with love. People get together and decide to marry because they love each other. No matter if the bride and groom are from different cultures or races, if they speak different languages, or come from a different social standing, everyone who gets married does so because of love. This thought always brought me comfort, knowing that I was playing a small part in their lives together and in the love they had for each other.

I think people appreciated my honesty and bluntness, as well as my charismatic personality. I had a lesbian couple getting married, and the first thing I asked them was, "Who wears the pants in this family?" They were not offended, and we got along very well. I was tempted to say, "I don't care what religion you are, everyone is welcome at Carmen's."

There are a few weddings that I will remember to the day I die. At one such wedding, I was standing at the back of the hall, listening to the groom speak. When I heard what I heard, I thought it was a joke, some kind of comedy skit. The groom thanked his father-in-law for the great party and then his best friend for banging his wife. He invited everyone to stay and enjoy themselves and then immediately left the hall, never to return. The bride was in disbelief, and most of the people started to clear out rather quickly.

At another wedding, a five-foot, 300-pound man was drinking, smoking and being crazy on the dance floor. His family was telling him to calm down or he would die. But he continued carrying on and, a few minutes later, he actually did drop dead.

We have had our share of disasters. At one wedding, a bridesmaid spilled red wine all over the bride's dress just before the bride was to enter the hall. The bride had a complete meltdown. We postponed the reception for an hour, allowing me time to call the wedding dress store and have them bring the bride another dress.

Another wedding turned out to be like a crime mystery. The best man did not show up. The amount of conversation and energy put into trying to figure out why he didn't show up played out like a Columbo movie. They managed to finally reach him after he returned home from a day of golfing. He felt terrible, having written down the wrong date in his time book.

The wedding day is supposed to be one of the happiest days in the life of a bride and her bridesmaids. At one wedding, we had a bridesmaid completely break down, sobbing and crying and not able to carry on, because her boyfriend broke up with her that day.

One day, I arrived home to shower and change before returning to the hall for a wedding. I received an unlikely call from Carla, our head banquet supervisor, asking me to return to the hall as soon as possible. I rushed back and was met by the father of the bride. He was as white as a ghost as he told me that the wedding was off. He explained how the groom came to his house in the morning, as his daughter was getting ready for the wedding, and informed him that he could not go through with the wedding. The father, still stunned and angry, left me and went to the church to explain to the people that the wedding was cancelled, but they were all invited to go to the hall and enjoy the food and drink. People from all over, including the USA, came to celebrate this wedding and the father wanted to express his appreciation.

People who arrived at the reception, who were not at the church, were shocked to hear the news. This did not deter them from having a great party. The father of the groom asked everyone to stay and enjoy themselves. Everyone took their place at the head table, minus the bride and groom, and they enjoyed a good meal and danced into the late evening.

A few days later, I received a call from the groom. He apologized to me and explained that he was not in love with his potential bride. He realized at the last moment that he was marrying her for all the wrong reasons.

At the planning meeting for one wedding, I had ten people show up: the bride and groom, the bride's mother and step-father, the bride's father and step-mother, the father and step-mother of the groom along with the groom's mother and step-father. I was anticipating a war and told them straight off that if there were any arguments, the meeting would end. I was pleasantly surprised to see that all eight parents were completely co-operative and were clearly there to support the bride and groom and each other. The wedding turned out beautifully.

At the time, Gaby and I had three beautiful children, Daniella and then PJ, who was born in 1980 and our youngest son, Joey, born in 1983. We were wrestling with the idea of whether or not to have more children. We were so happy with our three children and feeling grateful and content. Christina, a bride-to-be, came to organize her wedding. When I asked her what she did for a living, she told me that she worked in the part of the hospital where they did vasectomies. I shared with her that I was considering this procedure. Following some tough negotiations with her, wanting to get deals on a lot of our services, she handed me her card and asked me to call her if I decided to get a vasectomy.

Gaby and I talked about it again, and we decided that we were content and happy with the family we had and that I would go ahead with the vasectomy. I called Christina and the arrangements were made. While I sat in a waiting area in my hospital gown, with Christina nearby at the front desk, a rather large and daunting man entered the waiting area with a ten-inch knife. As he slowly approached me, I noticed he was sharpening this knife on a leather strap. Christina called out, "Peter, are you still going to give me those extra flowers with no cost?"

With a quivering voice, I answered, "Yes."

Then she asked, "Are you going to honour the discount on the desserts?"

I sheepishly answered, "Absolutely."

As the man now stood over me sharpening his knife, she asked, "And you're going to provide the colour of chair covers I want for free, right?"

Completely surrendering by this point, I yelled, "Yes!"

This daunting armed figure then turned around and exited the room. Thankfully, I was spared a castration and given my vasectomy.

Like any business, there were obstacles. Everyone wanted to get married on a Saturday. To fill the hall on Fridays and Sundays, we offered a twenty-percent discount. Business really boomed. My desire to learn everything and my competitive nature gave me that extra edge. I was never satisfied with just making good money. I always wanted to look ahead and build something bigger and better

– not out of greed, but because that's the way I'm wired. In addition, it was a great feeling to provide my wonderful team with more work and opportunities.

A lot of Muslims started migrating to the neighbourhoods around the banquet hall. They came to me with such a good offer, I was tempted to sell Carmen's to them. My wife quickly pointed out that I would go crazy with nothing to do and that we needed Carmen's for the children. The day would come when they would take it over, and their gifted business sense would make it better. Like most women, she had vision and was thinking of what would be best for me and the children.

As the expressways were built around our business and the Internet was growing, people started coming to our hall from all directions. One of the challenges faced by all halls is what to do with them during the week. With weddings and events happening from Friday to Sunday, the halls don't get much business from Monday to Thursday. Your fixed costs (mortgage, taxes, hydro, etc.) are there whether you are running events or not. Naturally, you want to try to offset those fixed costs during down times, so that the weekends are profitable. I wanted activities happening every day, so I looked for the "gap."

I realized that there were many seniors and elderly folks who were frequently looking for things to do. I decided I would come up with something to cater to this demographic in the afternoons from Monday to Thursday. I started booking tribute acts. These are shows where imitators sing the hits of the stars. It was a big hit, and seniors were coming to the hall in busloads throughout the week. The musical play *Grease* brought in 600 people a day for seven straight days. Six hundred tickets were sold, multiplied by $40 per ticket, brought in $24,000 a day. I filled the gap!

Years later, the casinos opened and started doing the same thing. All of the seniors flocked to Niagara, taking away our business. They paid entertainers twice the amount we paid and reduced their ticket prices. It completely killed this part of our business. I'm grateful for the great run we had and the opportunity to meet so many of our seniors and provide them with some enjoyment.

As you will see from my business model, a big part of success is determining what the "gap" is and filling it. We hosted many high-school graduations in our hall. I started to ask myself, "Why can't the elementary schools have gala graduations at my hall?" There are ten times the number of elementary schools as there are high schools. I approached a principal at a nearby elementary school and simply asked him, "Why should elementary school graduates be treated like second-class citizens compared to high-school graduates? Don't you want the very best for your kids?" It didn't take long before all the elementary schools were booking their graduations at Carmen's. We started a new trend in Hamilton. They were beautiful evenings, and I relished watching parents and grandparents coming to the graduations and watching their grandchildren with such pride as they graduated in splendour. I filled the gap!

I was always a fighter: striving to do good in school, being a good athlete and arm-wrestling champion, defending myself on the streets and fighting to be successful in business. In addition to predicting the trends and seeing the gaps, I think you also have to be a fighter. You must be willing to fight it out everyday, battling for every inch of ground you gain.

Carmen's Banquet & Convention Centre: una grandiosa festa per l'inaugurazione

Il sindaco di Hamilton tra gli ospiti d'onore

I tre proprietari del lussuoso centro per convegni e banchetti inaugurato ufficial-
mente ad Hamilton. Da sinistra, Morris, Peter e Sam Mercanti.

(Foto Corriere-G. Di Diodato)

di **G. Di Diodato**

HAMILTON - Giovedi' scorso ha avuto luogo la grande apertura ufficiale del Carmen's Banquet & Convention Centre. La serata ha avuto inizio alle ore 17 con un elegante cocktail e si é protratta fino alle 22 con musica dal vivo.

A questa simpatica manifestazione sono intervenute circa novecento persone del mondo del lavoro, della politica e della cultura che sono state intrattenute da numerosi artisti tra i quali i musicisti dell'orchestra "Matrix" e Fernando Viola che per l'occasione ha interpretato delle bellissime canzoni in italiano e in inglese.

Molti gli ospiti d'o-

nore intervenuti tra i quali il sindaco Bob Morrow, il Regional Chairman uscente Bill Sears e Monsignor Roach della chiesa di St. Francis Xavier.

Monsignor Roach ha benedetto la sala con una bellissima cerimonia religiosa dopo la quale il sindaco Bob Morrow, prendendo la parola, ha fatto tanti auguri ai proprietari del centro e li ha voluti elogiare per aver dato ad Hamilton il "Carmen's". Prima di lasciare il microfono, il sindaco ha donato un quadro raffigurante la citta' del ferro e la bandiera di Hamilton ai tre proprietari del locale, Sam, Peter, e Morris Mercanti.

Infine, i tre fratelli Mercanti hanno chiamato al microfono la sorella Rosanna e i genitori, Iolanda e Giuseppe Mercanti.

I tre fratelli hanno poi donato ai genitori un ritratto che li raffigurava ed hanno dedicato ad essi il locale.

Questo é stato un momento molto commovente per la famiglia Mercanti perche' si sono scambiati molti abbracci e c'é scappata pure qualche lacrima mostrando cosi' a tutti quanto sia grande e sacro l'affiatamento e l'attaccamento della famiglia italiana. A questo punto é esploso un lunghissimo e caloroso applauso da parte di tutti i presenti.

1987. Grand opening of Carmen's Banquet Hall

One day, I received a notice from SOCAN, demanding fees for the music played at my hall. As you may know, SOCAN is the organization that collects all the royalties from airplay of songs from radio and live performances in Canada. They distribute these royalties to the songwriters and publishers. Does that sound fair and reasonable to you? It does to me, but when it comes to banquet halls, I did not agree with their policies. I refused to pay the fees, making the argument that I already covered these fees when I paid a DJ or a band. I refused to pay twice. SOCAN would not comply, so I got a lawyer and fought my case. I won that case, forcing them to change the rules for me.

In addition to weddings, graduations and special events, we also brought in high-profile celebrities to support city charities. These events put Hamilton on the map with people such as: Michael Douglas, Al Pacino, Sylvester Stallone, President Bill Clinton, Dom DeLuise, Sophia Loren, Wayne Gretzky and many, many others. We called these shows, *Up Close and Personal*. Some of the celebrities would answer questions, others would give talks and others would put on a show.

Whenever I booked these high-profile celebrities, I would seek out sponsors for their shows. The sponsors would front the bulk of the money for the cost of the speaker. For example, Losani and Paletta contributed equally most of the money to pay Michael Douglas and Al Pacino their fees. For their generosity, the sponsors would be profiled and get to spend time with the celebrity and have their pictures taken with them. These were mostly fundraisers for charities, so they would also get a tax receipt. Tickets for these kinds of events were usually $150 and we would sell 800 tickets, bringing in $120,000. The advertising in our programs would bring in another

$20,000. With Michael Douglas, we made a profit of $150,000 and that went to support City Kidz, a great local organization. There were situations where the sponsors forged wonderful friendships with the celebrity, staying in touch with each other for years.

Life for me at Carmen's was absolutely wonderful in every way. It was exciting and adventurous, I was meeting people from all over the world and I was hosting events for some of the most important days in people's lives. But given my desire to keep moving forward to try different things, I did take on two hotels/centres in the heart of downtown Hamilton. But no matter how hard I tried, using every bit of hard work and creativity I could muster, I could not make it work. For many reasons, I could not get people to come downtown to my events. If you know the Hamilton of yesterday, you could appreciate this great obstacle.

From 2005 to 2007, Gabe Macaluso and I brought Cirque Niagara's production of *Avaia* from Russia to Niagara. Thanks to Gabe and our investors, Tony Battaglia, Paul Vacarello, Wayne Abbott, Igor Ineskinen, John Mitchell and several others, we managed to create a great show. It was a lot of work, including requiring me to go to Russia in order to bring back forty horses. In several shows we would fill a tent with 3,000 spectators. We offered the world's best acrobatic performances and the world's greatest theatrical equestrians. We wanted to give our spectators an experience that would captivate their senses, invigorate their soul and leave them feeling inspired.

I made money on this show, especially on the food and merchandise. It was a good run while it lasted. Niagara Parks Commission was getting more and more difficult to work with and, when the border started demanding passports, our attendance dropped by fifty percent. Shortly after, with rising gas prices and falling demand for the show, we backed out of the production.

Throughout the years, I really enjoyed going on trips with my friends, both business and recreational. Dennis Concordia, Frank DeNardis and I planned a trip to Milwaukee to attend a big Italian festival. It promised to be a great event. The three of us got on the plane and took our seats. Just prior to taking off I noticed Dennis was no longer in his seat. I asked the stewardess where my friend was and she said she thought he had gotten off the plane. We flew without him. As soon as we got to our hotel I called Dennis' wife to discover that Dennis has a fear of flying. Dennis showed up at the hotel the next day, explaining that he took five different puddle-jumper flights to get over his phobia of flying.

While in Milwaukee, I got the opportunity to meet the Chief of Police. The Chief told me that if I saw any officers during my visit I should tell them they were doing a good job. I went out of my way over the next few days to seek out every officer I could and told them that their chief said they were doing a great job. It may have irritated Dennis and Frank, but it sure made a lot of cops happy.

Throughout the years, I have been approached by individuals from all three levels of government, asking me to run for politics. In every case I turned them down. It didn't take much reflection to decide that politics wasn't for me. I told them that in my business I make roughly ninety-eight percent of my customers happy. If I became a politician, on my best day, I could only expect to make fifty percent of the people happy. The way I saw it, it would foolish to go from a ninety-eight-percent approval rating to a fifty-percent approval rating. Saying that, I have to say, I have great respect for politicians. They take criticism from every side, and no matter how hard they work and how well they do, they receive criticism and even insults from a large percentage of the population. I have great admiration for anyone that decides to become a public servant. I have made personal lifelong friendships with many politicians that have served federally, provincially and many, many municipally. But that life is not for me!

I chose the business I chose because I saw financial opportunity, providing a good life for my family. I also loved the food and catering business. Being Italian, food plays such an important and even critical role in our lives and the life of our families. Finally, it had a very fulfilling aspect, playing a role in making people's weddings and events special and getting to meet people from all over the world. There is great satisfaction in serving others, especially on the most important days of their lives. As noble as this work is, and as much as I always tried to be a virtuous person, it does not mean that I always lived the noble life.

None of us are perfect. We all make mistakes. This sometimes happens when we are flying high and all is going well. Perhaps we take our comfort and success for granted. Perhaps it is because ego gets the best of us and we believe we are somehow insulated from trouble. What it comes down to is that we are all human, and no matter how wealthy, healthy or powerful we may be, we can fall to temptation, sin and suffering. I am no different and have made my share of mistakes.

As I mention in my story, one of the greatest "falls from grace" is when we hurt the ones we love and who love us. I have done that. I have hurt those who I love the most. I never intended to hurt anyone but, I suppose I got so caught up in my career and myself that I was ignorant to their needs and feelings.

One of my regrets is that I do not believe I was the father I could have been. I attended many of my children's events and special occasions and tried to always be there when they needed me, but I feel I could have been there more. This may be the plight of every parent, always thinking they didn't do enough – especially a parent like myself who had to work days and evenings to be successful.

It's all about balance, and balance is a difficult thing to achieve. I started with nothing and was determined to provide for my family. I was determined to be successful. It was this demand that I put on myself, combined with my own ambition and determination that took me away from my family more often than I would have liked. To add to this regret, I believe, because of stress and my own weaknesses, there were times in which I was too impatient.

I urge young business people to always work at finding that balance. As the Buddha advises, "Take the middle path." It will involve a lot of work and effort on your part, but I guarantee you it is all worth it. Work hard, dedicate the time you need to build your career and business, but never at the expense of the ones you love. Success is important, but nothing is as important as love.

As much as we wish we can, none of us can turn back the clock. But the good news is that we are forgiven for our mistakes by God and by the people we love, even the ones we have hurt. This is the beauty and wonder of life – that we can be redeemed by the grace of God and others. Oh how wonderful my life became as I grew to see everything more clearly and find the intensity of love that brings true peace and happiness.

When we live our life righteously and with maturity, we wake up every morning with a pure heart and a clear mind. When we give in to temptation and fall to sin, we suffer greatly, as do those who love us most. We begin living life in confusion and chaos. When we finally wake up and see what we are doing, it is very difficult to find the forgiveness, even though we know that some of the greatest saints in history fell to these very temptations.

There can be some good that comes out of our human weakness. When we are stripped naked and brought to our knees, we look at life in a whole new way. The full realization of our own humanity causes us to see everything differently. For people like me, it is humbling and allows you to see and appreciate just how much you are loved by your family. As well, you are made to realize, at a whole new level, the depth of your love for them. When you experience these situations, you can choose to start the journey inward to examine yourself. You can look at yourself and all of life differently, beginning to value peace and everyday joy in a whole new way and realizing we all need each other's forgiveness and mercy at some point. Then we come to see just how critical it is to keep Jesus at our side. Out of darkness can come the warmth and beauty of light; out of suffering can come a whole new understanding of happiness; out of sin can come a great capacity for forgiveness; out of chaos and desperation can come a new life of peace. Saying this, I have to admit that I struggle to this day with the mistakes I have made and the people I have hurt. For this reason, I pray the Lord's Prayer every day and am fearless in continuing this journey within.

As Confucius said:

"The man who conquers a thousand armies is great,
but the man who conquers himself is greater."

I am determined to conquer myself.

It was also during my years at Carmen's that I became more and more sensitive to the plight of others and wanted to have as many fundraisers as possible to help the poor. My mind was made clear and my heart was opened wide by the poverty I saw in Africa and Bangladesh, along with the struggles I saw fellow Hamiltonians going through. I became intent on helping others. We did a lot of fundraisers for numerous charities, such as the Good Shepherd, Joy and Hope of Haiti, and our own organization, Charity of Hope.

I believe the poverty I saw in Africa later in my career had the greatest impact on me. Tony Cipolla, Dino Cortina and I went on a safari. I love animals, and this was also an opportunity for us to go on a man's trip. I watched a lioness hunt down a zebra but, after she made the kill for her and her cubs, she backed off to give way to the males who got first helpings. It troubled me to see how the animal kingdom is dominated by males while the females and children come second.

Tony and I dressed in a way that I would consider normal. On the other hand, Dino looked like he was going to a designer event. From his hat to his shoes, he was dressed as if we were going to a fashion show, surprising us every morning with a new outfit. We started calling him Designer Dino.

What was shocking to me was to see the depth and breadth of poverty among the people there. It consumed me. I would ask myself: *Is this for real? We supposedly live in a civilized world, and this is what exists?* These experiences influenced how I look at life to this day.

I hope you read at the beginning of the book my brother Sam's account of how "Charity of Hope" began. Sam explains how it all started with five-dollar donations from a few of us YMCA handball players to help a young immigrant teen and has now grown to be a life-changing charity for thousands of children in need. It is an honour for me to have served in the ways I could to support this charity through Carmen's. I urge you to visit the Charity of Hope website, and I thank you for supporting this charity through your purchase of this book.

Another fundraiser I have always been proud of is It's A Kids' Christmas. We hold this fundraiser in partnership with the Hamilton Police Services. It continued for thirty years with great success. Another fundraiser that was also a great success and was fascinating to observe was our Wild Game and Cigar Nights. You would watch the patrons take their places in the hall, the mob gathering in one area, the police in another and the businessmen in another. For one gentleman, one of these events marked his last good meal as he was arrested the next day. Many would later term it his "Last Supper."

When there was the devastating earthquake in Abruzzo in 2009, I assembled a crew of people to have a fundraising pasta night. More than 800 people attended this event. Our cousins Pat, Dino and Lidio from Sweet Paradise helped by supplying the buns and cannoli. This event created a ripple effect, causing every Italian group in Hamilton to hold their own fundraiser. Hamilton is a unique city, having many Italian groups, each representing a different part of Italy. How can anyone, especially me, not fall in love with this city and want to be an intimate part of its development? All of the groups formed an association and we pooled the proceeds. Angelo Di Ianni, Joe Mancinelli, myself and others went to Italy to be sure the $300,000 we raised was spent properly.

First annual "Wild Game and Cigar Night"

As the years passed, not only was I becoming a more integral part of this city I loved, I was, as I mentioned earlier, growing increasingly aware of the suffering of others and couldn't help but be sensitive to their plight. I wanted and had as many fundraisers as possible to serve those in need. I loved these events, bringing in the celebrities, meeting many Hamiltonians, being inspired by people's generosity and knowing I was doing my small part to make a difference. This desire to serve led to me becoming a founding member of the East Mountain Rotary Club. Rotary is an international organization whose purpose is to bring business and professional leaders together to serve the poor and bring peace around the world.

My Employees

Without a team of hard-working, loyal employees, it is very difficult to experience success. I have always been grateful to my employees. I am inspired by how hard they work and the sacrifices they make in their lives to support their families. I hope I have always been as good to my employees as they have been to me. I always tried to get to know my employees on a personal level, believing I might be able to help them in addition to the employment I offered. Perhaps, I would think, I could play a part in making their dreams come true. I would like to share a few of those stories.

Carla Sencic

Carla was our first employee and worked as a server/ supervisor. She set the standard for service at Carmen's. She trained every employee to ensure they provided top-quality service to our clients. Carla's exemplary work set the standard for the entire city and gave us our excellent reputation. Carla had an aura about her that was immediately recognizable, even by the most powerful politicians and superstar celebrities, whom she would always serve. They fell in love with her. What a blessing and a gift Carla was to Carmen's.

Danka Skokovic-Gates

I hired Danka to be our office manager. At the time, she was trying to get her parents out of a dangerous situation in Kosovo. I wanted to help, so we arranged a conversation with the Canadian Embassy in Kosovo. I awoke before 5:00 a.m. to make the call. The woman I spoke with said, "You must really like this person to call at 5:00 a.m." As it turned out, this woman was from Hamilton and knew about me and the Carmen's Group. Within a few days, Danka's parents arrived in Canada. What a wonderful feeling. Danka eventually went on to work for the Canada Revenue Agency.

Many employees at Carmen's met the love of their lives while with us and even got married. Ernie Moore, a very spiritual and righteous man, met his lovely Georgina at Carmen's. Everton

Moncrieffe and the beautiful Virgina also met at Carmen's and got married. Even my own son PJ met his future wife at Carmen's. I always took pride in how we were all one family at Carmen's. The atmosphere was one of hope and fellowship. I have been blessed to be a part of this environment and to had a hand in helping so many wonderful relationships form among these great people.

Carla Sensic, Everton Moncrieffe and Danka Skokovic
have been some of our greatest employees.

Cosetta Volpini

As my mother was aging and needed constant care, I turned to one of my favourite and most trusted employees, Cosetta Volpini. Our family needed someone who spoke Italian and had a caring and loving demeanour. We wanted someone who would care for her as if she were her own mother. Cosetta came to a meeting with the family and everyone loved her. Mom immediately fell in love with her when they met. We struck gold! Cosetta picked up Mom's spirits, changing her behaviour and attitude and making her happy. I am convinced that Cosetta lengthened my mother's life. After Mom passed away, Cosetta returned to work at the hotel. We are truly blessed to have this angel with us.

Saverio Carpino

Some employees are so different and unique that you find them intriguing. Their personality, the way they think and their spontaneity never ceases to entertain you. Saverio, a good-looking man who worked as a server, was a star basketball player at his school. We had a bride and groom plan their wedding with a basketball theme. I surprised them with a basketball net placed in the hall, and they watched as Savario dunked the ball. The groom followed in an attempt to match Saverio's talent. It didn't go too well for the groom.

Koco Polena

Koco is a strong, handsome man who can carry heavy trays with two fingers. I asked him what he did in his country, and he told me that he had worked in refrigeration. I asked him why he wasn't doing that here in Canada, and he told me that he wasn't certified. One day, I asked him to check my rooftop refrigeration unit. After watching him work on it, I realized he was a natural in this area. I called the president of Mohawk College, had him enrolled and paid for his education. After completing Mohawk's two-year program, Koco and I started a business together we called Ice Man Refrigeration Inc. After a couple of years, I gave him the business, and today he is very successful. We are grateful that Koco is still available to work on our systems.

I always got satisfaction and joy out of knowing that I offered people employment. It was important to me that my employees were receiving a good wage and able to make a life for themselves. As I have shared with you, I took special interest in the working and personal lives of my employees, wanting them to feel good about their work as well as their lives.

While providing employment at Carmen's, I believed that "you never plant anything in the shade of an oak." I viewed myself and Carmen's as the oak tree – a rather massive structure that cast a wide shadow. Although it keeps those sitting under it cool and comfortable, it stops the sun from shining on them and spurring their growth. I encouraged employees to follow their dreams, to stand out in the sun away from the oak and to grow. I encouraged and even helped some to set up their own businesses, while I paid for some to return to school. I wanted them to flourish in the area they were passionate about. I would often ask myself what I could do to push an employee with great potential out of the shade, to stand in the sun and grow like the oak they stand next to.

A Beautiful Young Man

As much as I desired to help employees, there is one situation that didn't turn out well. I hired the son of one of our employees. He was seventeen years old. At that time, I had about seventy people working at each event. When they would have a break, they would go off into groups to different spots on the property to relax. I noticed that this young man would always sit alone. I approached the boy and invited him to get something to eat and join his co-workers. He was personable and a beautiful young man, but he continued to choose to sit alone. I approached his mother to ask her about it and whether she felt okay about me approaching him to talk. She told me that he was a loner, despite her encouragement that he make friends, and that I should feel free to talk to him. I approached the boy again and continued to encourage him to socialize with the others. I knew something was wrong, but I wasn't sure what it was. A short time later, the boy took his own life. I wish I had done more, perhaps finding him a friend or a mentor at work. The memory of this beautiful young man haunts me to this day. It has given me a greater appreciation for mental illness and motivated me to be more willing to give to those who need help.

As George Bailey said: "All you can take with you is that which you've given away."

Carmen's continued to be very successful, but I began to sense the winds of change. My sons were bringing their own new and fresh ideas to the organization. One day, my son PJ approached me and suggested we build a hotel next to the banquet centre. Slowly, PJ was coming into the business, making his way and proving his abilities. I initially bucked his idea. We were almost free of our mortgage and I had bought out my brothers' shares. Just when I thought I could relax and watch profits begin to double, my son wanted to assume another mortgage to build the hotel. This was a stressful decision for me at the age of 61. Yet, PJ made a brilliant argument, pointing out that every time we had an event people wanted to know where the nearest hotels were. I felt the nudge, perhaps from God. PJ proved himself to be correct. Our hotel was built and soon became a roaring success, always filled to near-capacity and netting us many awards.

Chapter Ten

INGREDIENTS FOR GREAT LEADERSHIP

"Employees will work hard for a leader who has integrity and who truly loves them." P.M.

A good leader is ready for any situation. If you are in a leadership role, you will not only learn about people's personal skills and talents, you will learn almost every detail about their personal lives. You have to be there for your employees and react to every situation with calmness, prudence and justice. It's also important with the kinds of dilemmas you will face to have a sense of humour. I had an employee who was very good looking and built like a Greek god. He approached me and asked if I would do him a favour. He wanted me to hire more women because he had already dated every woman at Carmen's. His resources now exhausted, he was desperate for more opportunities. What could I do but laugh?

There are many leadership models out there. Some are service-based, others are driven by productivity and profits. I believe many of them to be great models that can be useful in executing your business. What I would like to *reveal* to you is my own leadership model, which I call **REVEAL.** It is my sincere hope that this model will serve you well in your own pursuits.

Leadership is a critically important ingredient to success. Some businesses will survive and even prosper under poor leadership if they have a widely desired product on offer. However, this is rare. In most cases, poor leadership will lead to the demise of a company. As well, poor leadership often saddles the proprietor with a terrible reputation, a despicable legacy – and an uneasy conscience.

My leadership model is based on more than productivity and profits. It is rooted in my personal philosophy of life and how I wish to conduct my relationships and my own behaviour. It is based on making me feel as good about myself as I can make my employees feel about themselves. Personally, I can't see any other way of leading. I hope you find **REVEAL** helpful.

With employees, you cannot be fake. You have to be who you are, always genuine and transparent. You must be like an open book because, if you are not genuine and you do not **REVEAL** who you truly are, they will not respect you. If they sense that you are just an actor trying to get as much out of them as you can, it will not turn out well for you or for your company. As tough as you have to be at times, do not be afraid to **REVEAL** who you truly are, to **REVEAL** your true character. You will gain your employees' respect, loyalty, honesty and even their friendship.

R – REFLECT

We can't allow our egos to ever get in the way of good leadership. Every great success begins and ends with good leadership. Putting our egos aside and adopting humility allows us to live each day with a clear mind and a pure heart. We will be able to take stock of each day with clarity and objectivity.

I think we can all agree that everyone makes mistakes. Even the wealthiest, most successful and the holiest of people make mistakes. None of us are perfect; we are all subject to error. We are challenged daily to put aside our egos and make the time to reflect on how the day has unfolded. We should be asking ourselves: What mistakes did I make today? Who did I help or hurt today? What could I have done better or different that would have benefited my employees or my business? Did I create a positive work environment, making my vision clear and bringing everyone together to accomplish our goals?

Making mistakes, as I have done many times, can make us better people, causing us to be more self-reflective. We have to make the time to reflect at the end of each day and summon the humility to admit our mistakes, the courage to correct them and then the fortitude to move forward and make the situation the best it can be.

This first step to good leadership may sound easy, but it isn't. It requires us to rise above self, abandoning the ego and taking the next step toward being more enlightened and, thereby, effective.

E – ENGAGE

Spending a lot of time getting to know your employees is critical to good leadership. It is easy to get wrapped up in the millions of details to be juggled and the profits we always have to keep an eye on. But we must never forget or neglect to find the time and make the effort to get to know our employees. We have to keep reminding ourselves that if not for these employees, there would be no business and no profits.

When we engage with our employees, we want to get to know them as well as their life stories. Everyone comes with their own life experiences, which shape those stories and who they are. Getting to know our employees on a deeper level helps us to understand them. We have to get to know their strengths, weaknesses and their potential. These are the members of our team and building a strong team is critical to success. In addition, our employees are often the people we choose to move into management. How do we make the right choice if we don't really know them and their personal as well as professional capabilities? Through spending the time to engage with them, we get to know them. We then know what we have to do and how to breathe confidence into them. Our leadership style must involve empowering them, elevating them to greater heights and getting them to see the potential in themselves.

It is critical to a business' success that we surround ourselves with a strong team, each member exercising their gifts in the right position to actualize success. It is critical that employees know we care about them, and this is demonstrated by how much time we spend engaging with them. They have to know that we will be diligent in doing what we can to empower them to exercise their abilities and actualize their gifts. When we do this, we are rewarded with great employees and managers who are efficient, effective but also happy. Never forget the tremendous personal satisfaction it will bring you to know that you are helping your employees to be the best they can be and how significant a contribution that is to them living the best lives they can live. When a businessperson assembles a team of strong and loyal employees, they will be one hundred percent on board with your vision and work tirelessly to make that vision a reality.

V – VALUES

Leadership is not easy. If it were, everyone would be a great leader. It is challenging and involves a lot of work. We previously spoke about the value of getting to know employees and working to make them the very best they can be. Leadership also involves getting to know and evaluating yourself. I believe that good leaders are values-based people. Really good leaders are people of good character. Therefore, as the leader of your company, you will want to put in the time assessing and building your own character.

Building personal character will benefit you, your employees and your family and friends. It sets an example to employees as to what you expect of them but also of the kind of people they can be. If you desire a virtuous employee, you should demonstrate kindness, friendship, honesty, courage, determination and other virtues. They will do the same. This will contribute to building self as well as your business.

There are many virtues that a leader should be focused on developing. Humility keeps us grounded and connected to every-one around us. It also creates the perfect environment for growth. Courage allows leaders to forge ahead, taking risks in empowering employees and moving the company forward. Wisdom and justice allow for prudent decision-making. They keep us focused on our vision, not just on profits. Empathy keeps us connected to all those we work with and plants the seeds of honesty and loyalty. Patience and perseverance keep the ship moving steadily and securely ahead, leaving the crew calm and confident that they are in good hands.

You may have your own list of virtues that guide you. What is important here is that we be a values-based person. Remember, it isn't just good for building a great company, it's good for our own sense of well-being and happiness.

E – EMPOWER

I have hired thousands of people over the years. Many of them were recent immigrants. The language barrier can lead you to question their skills and even their aptitude to learn the job and progress in it. I always tried to ignore that barrier. Being an immigrant who dealt with a language barrier myself, I saw first-hand how easy it is for others to misjudge a person's abilities. A good leader will go to great lengths to empower their employees. Not only will a good leader go the extra mile to provide the resources to empower employees, they will set expectations and demands on employees so that they can empower themselves.

There are many ways to empower employees. Regular recognition and affirmation of good work goes a long way. Offering new opportunities to them sends a clear signal that you believe in them. I've had employees who had a special gift or aptitude, and I would do whatever I could to help them achieve a dream. At the same time, I would set standards for them, so they could recognize their own abilities and talents when they succeeded in meeting those standards. They instinctively knew that I did this for their well being.

As you are now aware, in some cases I sent employees back to school and paid for their courses so they could embark on a whole new career. I didn't like losing them as employees, but it was what was best for them and their families. There were other employees I sent back to school, paying for their studies, who then returned to my company to manage an entire department. For others, I helped finance them starting their own company. Many of them did very well. For others, I got them better jobs at other companies and helped them to buy their first home. The joy this brought to me was more rewarding than looking at my bank account.

We have to be able to step past our own boundaries to help employees on personal as well as professional levels. These efforts will result in building great teams, a strong and loyal workforce and, most of all, a rich and rewarding life that's well worth living.

A – APPLY YOURSELF

Employees are not inspired by leaders who are never around or who have a poor work ethic. The ingredients I pointed out above indicate clearly just how much work is involved in being a good leader. And yet, there is still more work to do. Our employees have to witness just how committed and hard working we are. They have to be inspired by our work ethic, our commitment to our vision and our determination to see it all actualize. If employees do not see dedication and commitment in their leader, they will not be committed or dedicated. If employees do not see enthusiasm and passion in their leader, they will lack passion and enthusiasm.

We are all similar in that we are often motivated by the example others set. If we live in a society where everyone works hard, chances are we will be motivated to work hard. If we grow up in a family that values relationships, chances are we too will value relationships. If we have a leader who is enthusiastic, passionate, focused and hard working, chances are we will live out these traits as well.

I overheard one of my employees tell someone, "If you are in need, Peter will help you." I considered this a tremendous compliment. It warmed my heart and brought me a sense of pride. As leaders, we have to be in touch with and on top of every detail but also continually seeking the virtues that will make us the kind of leader that will not only inspire others but also build a business from nothing into something. We must apply ourselves every day to the task at hand, never losing sight of our larger vision. We must avoid getting too comfortable with our success or so full of ourselves that we lose sight of our larger goals.

L – LETTING GO

I believe that the inability to surrender and let go can destroy a family, personal relationships, businesses and one's very self. The ability to let go is critical to good leadership and to success in business. It's easy to say that you are letting something go, but it's never easy to do. It involves trying to understand a situation from every viewpoint and having the wisdom to recognize the truth of the matter, even if it makes you uncomfortable. It also involves having a forgiving heart.

You may have an employee who makes a terrible mistake. After addressing it, you have to be able to let it go. You won't make any progress by hanging it over the employee's head. It only creates animosity and will lead to disloyalty. If a business colleague or employee does something that hurts you in order to benefit themselves, you cannot dwell in anger or the desire for revenge. This can destroy you as well as your business. It will cloud your overall vision for your company and cripple your efforts to lead your employees.

Letting go does not mean becoming a doormat to others. It means remaining strong and determined while you cut ties with someone who did you wrong. However, do not allow having been wronged to lead you into becoming distracted by anger or thoughts of revenge. This is a bad example to set for your employees and will distract you and them from your mission.

Great leaders aren't always right, and sometimes they make mistakes. It takes greatness in a leader to admit to a mistake, rise above ego and be able to let go of the mistake. A great leader does not have to feel shame or try to keep it a secret when a poor decision has been made. Instead, a great leader becomes more clever, like a fox, knowing their environment and better understanding the jungle they are in. When a great leader loses almost everything to an unscrupulous person, they do not give up. Instead, they take the lesson and become wiser about the jungle. They find the courage to move forward and make better choices with their newly won wisdom. These qualities will impress and inspire your employees, as well as all those you do business with.

I have failed as many times as I have succeeded. I have been taken for lots of money, and I've loaned out lots of money that was never paid back. I have been lied to, cheated and taken advantage of. However, I have never allowed any of it to destroy me. What is important is that I continue to lead my employees forward, free of all the poison. I forgive and continue to wish everyone well, even though they did what they did. I am able to let go.

Resentment can overwhelm a person. It is bad energy. With resentment comes a mind that is imprisoned. It causes you to burn good energy to a bad end. Just say to yourself, "Let it go," and the next day, it will be gone. Don't let your ego get caught up in it and throw you off your game. Work at getting out of that bad zone. Remember, your employees are watching you and following your example. You are their leader; they *will* emulate you. Show them your ability to forgive and forge ahead, remaining focused on your vision.

THE SOPRANOS

SYLVESTER STALLONE

LIDIA BASTIANICH

TONY BENNETT

SARAH PALIN

BILL CLINTON

ANGELO MOSCA

SHIMON PERES

PAUL HENDERSON

ROY ORBISON

AL PACINO

GERRY DEE

SOPHIA LOREN

CHICAGO (THE BAND)

OLIVIA NEWTON-JOHN

DOUG GILMOUR

GOVERNOR MARIO CUOMO

Chapter Eleven

CARMEN'S CELEBRITY GUESTS

"Life is easier when you're genuine.
You don't have to fool anyone, especially yourself." P.M.

To get a celebrity to headline an event or fundraiser is no easy task. You have to deal with agents who are ferociously protective of their clients, legal documents that protect every aspect of a client and about one million other logistics. However, once the negotiations are done and the contracts are signed, it is usually pretty smooth sailing.

Whether it's a couple getting married, a group running a special event or a celebrity making an appearance, I wanted everyone to feel comfortable from the moment we met. If we were picking them up in a limousine, I would have homemade Italian panini and pastries waiting for them in the limo. They were always greeted at the entrance of our establishment with open arms. I wanted them to feel and know that this was more than just an event; they were now part of the Mercanti family. None of this was an act. It was sincere. That is truly how I felt toward everyone who walked through our doors. They were special, and we felt special hosting them.

If my work was strictly about business and making profits, I would not have enjoyed any of it. I loved meeting new people, welcoming them into my home and forming some kind of friendship with them. It was this aspect of my work that kept me energetic and fulfilled for thirty-five years. It took a team effort and a lot of work to make these events happen. I owe a lot to my dear friend Dennis Concordia for making all of this a reality. He was instrumental in securing many of the celebrities and attending to every detail to ensure the evenings were a great success.

Here are just some of the celebrities I got to meet. Although I was only able to spend a short period of time with them, I loved every minute of it. The evenings were called:

"Up Close and Personal With…"

Al Pacino

Our committee knew from the beginning that securing Al Pacino for an event at Carmen's would not be an easy task. In the process of making connections and supporters I was introduced to Frank D'Angelo of D'Angelo Foods. As two Italian entrepreneurs in the food business, we immediately hit it off. Frank became a big supporter as well as one of the sponsors of this event to make it all happen.

We hosted Al Pacino at Carmen's as well as in Windsor and Toronto. The format of the evening was a question-and-answer session led by a moderator. He was just phenomenal – funny, accommodating and cordial. I so appreciated spending that little bit of time that I did with Al.

Whenever you have a celebrity headline an event, their agent sends you a long list, sometimes two pages, of all their needs and requirements, right down to the menu. It took five years to secure

Pacino, and as soon as we thought we had the deal secured, we ran into a glitch. His agent informed us that Al would not sit at the head table. In addition to being a movie star, Pacino is a theatre actor. He likes to get in the mood and prepare mentally before a performance. His agent told us that he couldn't prepare if he was sitting at the head table throughout the meal. I got upset and threatened to cancel the event. However, upon reflection, I realized how many people had worked on this event, all the planning and organization that had gone into making it happen and all those who were ecstatic at the thought of him coming to Hamilton. So, I compromised and agreed that Pacino didn't have to sit at the head table.

When you bring in stars like Pacino, an awful lot of people want to get tickets. From the wealthy to those struggling to make ends meet, from everyday working people to celebrities in their own right, everyone wants to be there.

We set up a special area on the balcony for Al and his group. We had his food, as specified by his contract, spread out on his own table, as requested. His staff ate the food from a separate table that we had also set up. As Al walked toward his table, he saw lasagna on the staff table. His eyes locked on that lasagna. Ignoring the food set out for him, he asked if he could have some of the lasagna. "Of course, of course," I told him. Not only did he eat the lasagna as if it was the last available food on Earth, he almost licked the plate! At his request, I gave him a large serving of lasagna to take on his flight home and then I had to courier lasagna to his home in New York for some time.

https://www.thespec.com/news/hamilton-region/2010/11/24/
pacino-s-hamilton-souvenir-carmen-s-homemade-lasagna.html

Left: Peter and Al Pacino

*Right: I had to keep a close eye on my
daughter as her and the Godfather/Scarface
were having a moment.*

Brothers Morris, Peter and Sam greeting Sophia Loren

Sophia Loren

Sophia Loren is one of the classiest and most elegant, humble and beautiful women I have ever met. When I first saw her, I was shocked at how tall she is. With my shorter stature, I was at eye contact with her breasts. (I had an enchanting conversation with both of them!) When I was able, through great discipline and determination, I raised my head and made eye contact. I couldn't get over, even at the age of 65, how beautiful she is. More impressive was her humility and down-to-earth demeanour.

Sophia talked about Italy and how she liked visiting Toronto to see Italy again. She would go to Toronto because Italians that came over from Italy had a tendency to preserve the culture they had left behind. Italy had changed dramatically, becoming so Americanized, so Toronto had become the place to see the "real" Italy.

One of our sponsors for this event was an extremely wealthy man, worth tens if not hundreds of millions of dollars. He had had a lot to drink and when he met Sophia he was so stunned by her beauty that his eyes began to roll back in his head. He said to her, "I am wealthy, single and own my jet that will fly you anywhere you want." Sophia, in a very classy and gracious way, let him know that she was grateful for his flattery but not interested.

Sylvester Stallone

We ran into a rather serious glitch when we booked Sly Stallone. After we had booked him, his agent then booked him at a casino in Niagara. Because our establishment was within fifty kilometres and the casino did not allow Stallone to perform within a fifty-kilometre range of their casino, they demanded that he cancel the booking with Carmen's. I was enraged and threatened them with a head-line in the *Spectator* saying something to the effect that the Ontario Lottery Corporation was willing to block a charity event to benefit children. The provincial government caved, and Stallone honoured our booking.

With Stallone, we had the likes of investor and TV personality Robert Herjavec call to ask for tickets. At our invitation, he was happy to sit at the head table.

He was a class act. He was respectful, gentle, soft-spoken and insatiably curious. He stayed at our hotel in the Stallone Room (named after him). I was privileged to have breakfast with him the next day. I was shocked to see, once he took off his jacket, the shape he was in – he has big hands, large arms and is positively ripped. He had just finished filming *The Expendables 2*.

Stallone loved our hotel and, over dinner, he had a barrage of questions for me. I couldn't get over how interested he was in my life and my business. He had invested in some restaurants in the U.S. and wanted to know a lot about how my business was doing. I kept trying to talk about his movies and his life, and he would constantly redirect the conversation back to me. I finally managed to ask him what it was that motivated him and he simply replied, "This is my role in life."

Left: "One-Punch Pete" giving Stallone some tips
Right: Angelo Paletta, Robert Herjavec and myself with Stallone

Michael Douglas

At the time of the Michael Douglas event, the City of Hamilton was opening the new Red Hill Valley Expressway, and they had organized a marathon run up the expressway to mark the event. We hosted Michael Douglas that evening to raise money for CityKidz, an organization in town that helps inner-city children and youth.

Initially, Michael did not want to sit at the head table nor wear a poppy, even though it was November and near Remembrance Day.

He eventually agreed to both. Normally, Michael never spoke in public, and he was very nervous before the event. He was so nervous that he came with his own audio technician to operate the video that was to play during his talk. They held an afternoon rehearsal and everything went perfectly. When it was time for him to speak, the video wouldn't play. He kept clicking the clicker but to no avail. In spite of this glitch, Michael gave a great talk and the audience loved him. As it turns out, he had accidentally hit the wrong button, and it muted the entire video.

PJ and Michael Douglas

"The Great One" / Wayne Gretzky

Wayne Gretzky

What an honour to have Wayne with us here. My time spent with him was very limited but to have had him here was a privilege. He is considered by many to be the greatest hockey player of all time and the National Hockey League's top scorer. At the time of his retirement, he held a staggering sixty-one NHL records.

Paul Henderson

One summer, my wife and children and I were vacationing in the Muskoka. While eating lunch one day, my son PJ grabbed my arm and said, "Look, Dad, there's Paul Henderson!" I looked over, nodded and said, "Yes, but let's not bother him." Paul Henderson played thirteen seasons in the NHL and five seasons in the World Hockey Association. He had a fantastic career but is best known for scoring the winning goal in the 1972 game where Canada beat the Russians. That goal was voted the "Sports Moment of the Century" by the Canadian Press. PJ hadn't even been born when Henderson made that goal, yet he is such a sports and Canadian icon that even PJ knew who he was.

Paul must have overheard us talking about him because he came over to our table and introduced himself. After eating lunch together, he invited me to play a round of golf with him. What a perfect gentleman and a truly Christian man. He invited me to stay in touch and we did.

PJ was in high school, and it was his job to get a good public speaker to come to the school and motivate and inspire the students. He called Paul who agreed on the condition that we, as a family, have lunch together at our house. It turned out to be wonderful. Some time later, I called Paul to speak at a golf tournament fundraiser. He

agreed, and it was another great success. In addition to his friendship, Paul has been a great source of inspiration and counsel for me.
He has had an even greater impact on my brother, Sam. I think
it is safe to say that Paul changed Sam's life in a significant way,
with Sam now getting up every morning at 5:30 a.m. to pray. Sam
continues to run two leadership and Bible groups that are focused
on living the life Jesus wants us to live. Paul's morals, high standards
and exemplary behaviour make him a very special human being.

Dom DeLuise

What you saw on TV is real – Dom DeLuise is always joyful, smiling
and a delight to be with. You couldn't ask for a nicer guy. Rather
than doing a question-and-answer segment, he gave a cooking dem-
onstration. Prior to the show, everyone in the audience was given
expensive utensils to use for the food he cooked and served. At the
end of the meal, he gladly announced to the audience that they
could take home all my expensive silver utensils they were using. The
audience cheered, clapped and laughed as I stood at the back of the
hall and cried.

Dom DeLuise never stops smiling

Bill Clinton

Carmen's was the first place in all of Canada to book President Bill Clinton. The media coverage across Canada was phenomenal, and it was a good feeling to beat out the Toronto bidders. The security detail that arrived weeks before the event studied every square foot of our facility, including the roof, parking lot and surrounding area. The RCMP and FBI worked together to guarantee a secure and safe evening for Clinton. There were numerous meetings prior to the event involving security, tickets, pricing, marketing and the evening itself.

When Clinton arrived, he entered through the back door, stopping to greet the kitchen staff and have his picture taken with them. One of our staff was a Christian from Iraq who was overwhelmed with pride and joy to have his photo taken with the former President. He pointed out that if the people of Iraq were to see the photo, his entire family would likely be massacred.

I was personally taken aback to see that one of Clinton's aides that evening looked identical to Monica Lewinsky, the intern who had caused him so much trouble while in office. Clinton is a tall, good-looking man who was courteous to everyone and allowed photos to be taken with anyone who asked. He gave a great speech, and the night was a wonderful success. There was only one glitch that evening – one of the security agents who was watching the surrounding area from our rooftop spotted a man with a bow and arrow in the field across from the Centre. The police were called, but all eventually was calm again when it was discovered he was merely hunting.

My son Joey, a teenager at the time, served Bill Clinton his dinner. Our top-notch employee and instructor Carla Sensic trained Joey how to serve. It's a good thing she did or the steak may have ended up on Clinton's lap.

Joey serving Bill Clinton

My beautiful wife and I with Bill Clinton

George H.W. Bush

It was an honour to host the forty-first President of the United States at Carmen's. He was a politician, diplomat and businessman who had also served in the navy. He navigated the final years of the Cold War and played an important role in the reunification of Germany. In addition to having served as president, Bush served in many other significant capacities, including ambassador to the United Nations, chairman of the Republican National Committee, chief of the Liaison Office to China, and Director of Central Intelligence.

My beautiful daughter Daniella, my gorgeous wife
Gabriella and myself with George Bush

Jean Chretien

Chretien served as the twentieth Prime Minister of Canada. Under Prime Minister Pierre Trudeau, Chretien served as Minister of Justice, Minister of Finance and Minister of Indian Affairs. Chretien had a wonderful personality, always smiling and friendly. He loved our venue and Carmen's Banquet Hall.

My wife Gabriella and Jean Chretien

Tony Bennett

What an honour to have an icon and talent like Tony Bennett come to our establishment. You would think it would have been the perfect event, but that was not the case. My twelve-year-old grandson and I arrived at the airport in our limousine to pick him up. Before I even met Bennett, his agent rushed forward to inform me that we were to sit across from him in the limo. All the way back to Hamilton, very few words were spoken. Bennett and his agent were about as distant and stoic as can be. It was one of the longest hours in my life.

Although Bennett contractually agreed to sign autographs and have pictures taken, his agent quickly pointed out that he wanted no part of it. I responded sternly that they agreed to sign autographs and have pictures taken during the performance. The agent also told our photographer to stop taking pictures. During the performance I had strong words with the agent in the kitchen, telling him I expected him to honour his contract. I used language inappropriate for this book. Needless to say, I put this arrogant and rude agent in his place. I also told him to take some of his commission and buy manners with it.

Most upsetting was when I discovered that Bennett sang "I Left My Heart in San Francisco" while I was arguing with the agent. That is my favourite Bennett song.

I believe I am accommodating to celebrities and to everyone in every way possible. However, I have integrity and will not be pushed around. I will not tolerate any agent's arrogance, ignorance or non-sense, particularly in the presence of my grandson.

"He left his heart in San Francisco" – Tony Bennett

Sarah Palin

In order to host Sarah Palin, we partnered with a major local health-care provider. There was a lot of controversy regarding her visit to Hamilton. Many people were opposed to her coming for political reasons but mostly because she wasn't in favour of universal health-care. There was so much controversy that the healthcare provider backed out of their sponsorship. Once they had dropped out, ticket sales began to tank. Tom Weisz loved Palin, and he stepped in as co-sponsor, along with my brother Sam. All the proceeds from this successful event went to the Charity of Hope.

We had many local politicians calling, anxious to meet her. Sarah had some trepidation given the amount of controversy that had developed. The story even made headlines in Alaska. Despite the amount of security we had, she brought her husband so she would feel even more safe and secure.

I'm happy to share with you that there are still people from my past who recall and appreciate my singing ability. At their suggestion, I sang the "Star-Spangled Banner" that evening, and Sarah said she loved it. It was an honour for me to do so, not to mention a boost to my ego. I asked Sarah if she would start her talk by saying that she was a friend of Hamilton and that she supported the city's bid for an NHL team. She was happy to do it.

The event went off really well, except for one glitch. Part of her contract did not allow any taping of the show. A journalist hid a recorder and taped the event, later releasing it to the public. Sarah Palin gave a great speech and I found her to be kind, accommodating and a real class act.

Dennis Concordia, Ernie Moore and myself with Sarah Palin

Olivia Newton-John

Olivia was one of the most beautiful celebrities I have ever met. Outside of her physical beauty, she is humble, kind and a real class act. Her presentation was powerful, talking about her life and her bout with cancer. She was gracious with the question-and-answer period, and the people loved her. You would never believe that she was a superstar. I was honoured to have her stay in our hotel and to have breakfast with her the next day before she departed.

The inspiring, beautiful Olivia Newton-John

Olivia Newton John was so happy to be with us at Carmen's. She asked me if she could
have a private conversation with one of our event managers, Charlie Agro, when she discovered
he had a Masters of Theology. It was a defining moment that captured her thirst for spiritual
questions and made her forget the VIP event was all about her.

Margaret Thatcher

We hosted Margaret Thatcher, Britain's first female Prime Minister, at the Canadian Warplane Heritage Museum. Thatcher was one of our very first guests, and her appearance brought a lot of credibility to Carmen's. When you book celebrities, they will check you out before they agree to come. You have to have a proven track record and a solid reputation. Although Margaret Thatcher was very stoic and appeared to be a tough woman, she was kind, gentle and very professional.

Left to Right: Galen Weston, Margaret Thatcher, Morgan Firestone

Phyllis Diller

The Phyllis Diller you saw on television was the Phyllis Diller you met in real life. She was funny, funny and funnier. She had boundless energy and was full of life and humour. She was such fun to spend time with.

Near the end of her presentation she had forgotten her lines and said; "Ah f--k, I forgot what I was going to say. I'm sorry. Thank you. Have a good day." It was the perfect funny ending to a perfect funny evening.

Phyllis Diller: Hilarious, hilarious and more hilarious

Lidia Bastianich

Lidia was such a great guest we had to have her back a second time. She is an absolutely beautiful person, full of life and joy. We built her a stage and brought in her chef from Kansas City so that she could create one of her Lidia-inspired meals. She was such a gracious guest, receiving and answering every question from the audience.

The money raised from this evening went toward purchasing trauma-room equipment for one of our local hospitals.

Sam, myself and Lidia Bastianich

The Mamas & The Papas

The agent for The Mamas & The Papas came in with the band early in the morning to introduce them to me. I was shocked to discover that the entire band was stoned. I became anxious, worried that they would put on a terrible show or perhaps not even show up. I discovered that evening that once they got on stage, stoned or sober, they were absolutely magical.

Public Enemy

I rented our hall to a promoter who booked Public Enemy. I had no idea who he was bringing in. I put things together rather quickly when the police chief contacted me. I called the promoter and told him I wanted to cancel the event. He was co-operative but, when he contacted the group in New York, they immediately responded (via my fax machine) with hundreds of pages threatening a lawsuit. I immediately contacted my lawyer, but soon realized that they had me over a barrel.

On the night of the concert, everyone was frisked at the door, and there were many guns and knives discovered. Members of Public Enemy approached me, including Flavor Flav, trying to intimidate me because I hadn't wanted to host the event. I didn't have any patience for this nonsense or their big silly clocks that hung around their necks. I told them to just behave themselves.

Chicago

They were probably the nicest group of band members we ever booked. As we all know, their music is phenomenal, leaving their spectators awestruck. They had a way about them that made the event feel like an intimate party. This fundraiser, which raised a lot of money, was for the Good Shepherd, spearheaded by Cathy Wellwood.

Gaby and I after celebrating an evening with Chicago

The Four Lads

Tony Busseri, brother of Frank Busseri of the Four Lads, approached me one day and asked me if I would listen to a tape. After listening, I realized how great and successful the Four Lads were. At his request, I booked them, and they were a phenomenal success with the seniors in our afternoon shows. Tony became their agent and started ARB Productions. Tony and his brother were such wonderful people – professional, talented and a joy to work with.

Mario Cuomo

Of the hundreds of speakers we have had, New York Governor Mario Cuomo was the most eloquent. When he spoke, you could hear a pin drop in that banquet room. When I met him personally, he was especially interested in the part of Italy I came from. We spoke about all things Italian. Our head supervisor Carla Sensic said that Governor Cuomo was her favourite guest.

Morris, Sam and I with the greatest public speaker
who graced Carmen's: Mario Cuomo

James Woods

James came to Carmen's for an event sponsored by CARSTAR. He stayed at our hotel. Maybe because he acted in a lot of mob movies he thought he was a good poker player. We were happy to play a game of poker with him. He ended up the first to be beaten.

James is a fabulous guy, taking photos and signing autographs for everyone who asked. In terms of being accommodating and fun to be with, he was probably the best celebrity we had. He made friends with the people here and to this day some stay in touch with him.

Sam Mercanti (Canada CARSTAR founder), myself and James Woods, one of the friendliest and most accommodating celebrities ever, but a lousy poker player

Fran Tarkenton

What a gentleman and classy guy. Fran is also a strong Christian. He was our guest speaker at one of our annual CYO celebrity events and delivered a wonderful and inspiring message. Shortly after the event, I received a call from Craig Dowhaniuk telling me to get ready to catch a plane for Georgia. He wouldn't tell me what it was for. After touching down in Georgia, we were driven to a swanky hotel and ended up playing golf at Augusta National Golf Club. This was all arranged for us by Fran Tarkenton.

I played a terrible game of golf. I asked the caddie, who was a person of colour, how he found the course when he played on it. He told me that he had walked that course for twenty years and hundreds of times but never played on it. I told him to take a few shots. He emphatically declined, saying he would be fired if he got caught playing. I insisted he try a few shots and that I would not continue until he did. I reassured him that nobody was looking, and I was determined to see if I could learn what I was doing wrong regarding this course. He finally caved. We enjoyed playing the last couple of holes together.

Al Martino

When Al Martino entered Carmen's, the first words he uttered were, "Where's your kitchen? I want to cook my own food." We escorted him to the kitchen and then stepped back, watching him survey the entire kitchen. He then commented, "Big f%$* kitchen. How do you find anything here?" I instructed our chef to show Al where everything was. After examining our supplies he asked, "Where's an Italian supermarket around here?" We drove him to Fortinos and as soon as he returned with groceries in hand he put on his apron and started cooking. He cooked up a fantastic pasta meal and invited us to join him.

Al gave a great performance, singing and telling stories. His audience was especially interested in his stories regarding the filming of *The Godfather* and his role in the film.

Al Martino performed at Carmen's more than any other guest. From 1993 to 2009, Al had performed over twenty times.

Gabriella, myself and the famous Al Martino

The Sopranos

When *The Sopranos* TV show was a big hit, people would often socialize at each other's homes to watch the show. Gabe Macaluso and I went to New York City where Gabe arranged a meeting with the very popular Gumba Johnny. Gumba managed to get us a meeting with *The Sopranos'* agent. Negotiations pursued, and we managed to book the stars of *The Sopranos*.

As soon as we announced this fundraising event for a charity, our phones started ringing off the hook. Getting sponsors to cover the cost of hosting *The Sopranos* stars was rather easy. People love them and wanted to meet them and have pictures taken.

The event was like a Hollywood premiere and a phenomenal success. They were a great bunch of guys, answering every question, visiting all the tables and being very accommodating to all our patrons.

My family and "The Sopranos"

Mickey Rooney

I felt tall standing next to Mickey Rooney. Women went crazy over him, and they were lined up to get his autograph. Mickey Rooney wasn't the nice guy you saw in some of his movies. He was miserable and refused to sign anything if you didn't buy his book or picture. Enough said about him.

Rudy Ruettiger

Rudy is a Notre Dame legend, wearing #45 and inspiring the motivational movie entitled *Rudy*. It was one of my all-time favourite films. He was booked for another one of our CYO celebrity dinners. He was small in stature but a giant of a man. I told him that I watched his movie five times. Rudy was the only celebrity I was taller than.

Domenic Primucci

The BEA (Business Excellence Awards) honours fifteen people annually for their business accomplishments. CIBPA (Canadian Italian Business Professional Association) hosted the event at Carmen's. Domenic Primucci was guest speaker at one of these events. Domenic was born to immigrant parents from Italy. His father and uncles opened a small pizzeria in 1963. They called it Pizza Nova. It has grown into having over 150 locations. Domenic is a smart, charismatic businessman, along with being a great family man.

Shimon Peres

Because the times were so turbulent in the Middle East, when Shimon Peres, the former Prime Minister of Israel visited, there was a very heavy security detail. He had six agents standing in front of him while he was on stage. One of them was sweating so profusely I approached him to offer him some water. He refused. After the presentation and Peres was off-stage, the security guard apologized to me for being so blunt. He informed me that if something happened to his leader during the presentation, and he was distracted by drinking water, he could never return to his country.

Another Talented Woman

Chantal Kreviazuk at a Charity of Hope fundraiser

My Favourite Celebrity, My Dad

Of all the celebrities and politicians that graced Carmen's Banquet Hall, there is one person who impressed me more than any other and was certainly more entertaining. He wasn't famous or wealthy and did not hold a position of power. He did not come to Carmen's as someone famous who would entertain the guests, but for me, in my heart and mind, he was the most impressive and entertaining. Let me share with you just one story about my dad and you will understand what I mean.

My father, like most Italians, loved his modest garden. He had a small yard, but he cared for it like it was a hundred acres. One day, when I went to visit Mom and Dad, Mom was in the kitchen making lasagna and Dad was in the backyard. When I went out to see him, I was shocked to see him sitting in the yard with his hunting rifle on his lap. Rather upset and worried, I asked him what the hell he was doing with his rifle. He explained to me in Italian that he was guarding his garden.

With such a small yard, he didn't have much of a garden but he was determined to protect his tomatoes, cucumbers, carrots, lettuce and his fruit tree from enemies. The enemy he kept a special eye out for were the squirrels. As I tried to convince him that he shouldn't be doing this and he can't have a gun in the city, a squirrel ran along the fence line. He quickly raised his rifle, took his sniper pose, aimed and shot it dead. I jumped back and yelled, "Are you nuts!?"

Dad ignored my opposition and let out a deafening whistle that could be heard throughout the neighbourhood. When I asked what that whistle was all about he simply responded, "Don't worry." Within a few minutes, a young boy who lived in the neighbourhood came running into the backyard with a sack and bagged the squirrel. My father then gave him five dollars. He turned to me and said, "I trained him to come and get the dead squirrels."

I am grateful for the neighbours who were extremely patient with my father. Not only did they tolerate the random gun fire, they tolerated his thirty chickens and forty pigeons that he kept in a small wooden shed at the back of the yard. Dad got a thrill when he took his pigeons twenty miles from home, released them, and they always found their way back home. The neighbours were never thrilled with the crap these pigeons would drop on their cars and house roofs, but they tolerated it because they liked Dad.

Chapter Twelve

INGREDIENTS FOR BUSINESS SUCCESS

"Work and grow until the day you die." P.M.

Business is the ultimate challenge. It is the ultimate competition. Some say you have to be born with that competitive gene. Others will say that the desire to be an entrepreneur can be acquired by growing up in a business family. Others will say poverty can be the motivating force. I'm not sure what the cause or source is, but it is an exciting and wonderful life. It provided me the opportunity to make a good living, the freedom to be my own boss and it allowed me to do it "my way."

Upon reflection, I sometimes wonder if I was too competitive. I think back to when we were playing handball at the YMCA and just how competitive I was. Anthony Rizzuto and Marco Faiazza played racket ball. I would constantly tease them, saying, "What kind of men are you. Real men play handball. Only women play racket ball." Upon Anthony's request I taught him to play handball. He got good fast and before he could beat me, I stopped playing him.

My competitive nature showed itself again when I refused to continue arm wrestling with my 6000-calorie-a-day, body-building grandson. Once again, I would not allow myself to be beaten.

As competitive as I was, I have always believed that any negotiations must end in a win-win situation. It's not good for either side of a negotiation to feel like someone was beaten for their money. You have to adopt the attitude of working co-operatively and be able to compromise so that both parties come out winners. Bad deals only result in bad karma. Just remember – be willing to compromise all things except your integrity.

When you enter a negotiation, start with the attitude that both of you have to eat. Both parties are struggling to make a go of it, so a win-win result is the best goal to set. Go in prepared and extremely organized, knowing every aspect of your business. If you don't have all the facts, you risk being manipulated. As well, be willing to walk away if things are just not going your way. Be transparent with each other, respect each other and be fair to each other. Ask yourself, "How would Jesus play this game?" He wouldn't cheat someone. He would be fair.

I call my Business plan for success **The 12 Plus 12 Plan.** Success involves business ingredients as well as personal ingredients, both working together to accomplish the goal.

Personal Ingredients

1. A strong desire to be your own boss and your own person without others telling you what to do everyday. This desire to "fly on your own" will motivate you through the difficult times.

2. Getting a sense of pride and accomplishment from earning your own money in your own way. This affinity for autonomy will also push you through the difficult times.

3. Have a competitive nature combined with self-confidence and a belief that you can do whatever you dream of doing. Being naturally competitive will allow you to fly in any direction, while solid self-confidence will overshadow any fear you may have.

4. A positive attitude is critical; you must believe in what you are doing and that it will work no matter what happens. Further, you must remain positive and undefeated – even when you have been defeated! This is not only critical to your own success but to that of those around you because people want to surround themselves with positive thinkers.

5. You must have the ability to acknowledge your talents and abilities and a strong desire to make the best of them. Many recognize their potential but go through life flat-lined, never actualizing their gifts. None of us is super human, but we have to be willing to take what we have and make it great.

6. Go into every meeting, negotiation and business venture with the intent that you and your negotiating partner will both WIN! You must first see yourself as a winner; never allow a poor self-image or negative baggage to get in the way of believing in yourself.

7. You must never be a quitter. Even if you don't win, if you go bankrupt or get destroyed, be the type of person that keeps getting up. Giving up is the easy

way out. When the bell rings, you have to get up from your corner to fight another round.

"Success is the ability to go from one failure to another with no loss of enthusiasm."
—Sir Winston Churchill

8. Have no fear to stand up and face the beast. A degree of fear may be healthy, but it must never be your master. You are like the wolverine – not even a bear will chase you away. If you lose a battle, be willing to start over, change direction or try something entirely different.

9. A business life can be riddled with stress, and you have to be able to manage that stress. Otherwise, it will end up managing you. Some stress can be enjoyable with the adrenaline rush it can send through your body.

10. Be prepared for your business life to spill over into every aspect of your life. You must be the type of person who can compartmentalize, not allowing business concerns to impede on your family life, friendships or spiritual health. Never allow it to take away your positive attitude or cheerfulness from any aspect of your life.

11. Commit yourself to remaining true to your values. Never allow money to be your master. Remember, you are driven by the project or product and believe

you are offering your clients something wonderful. Always remain ethical!

12. You must hate losing. This may sound obvious, but it is not. An amazing number of people have such low self-esteem that, deep down, they don't mind losing. They don't feel worthy of success and, as much as they say they want to win, negative baggage will send them the message that they are only worthy of losing.

Business Ingredients

1. You must provide a service people want to buy. No matter how much you love something or performing a particular function, if nobody wants to buy what you offer, your business is in trouble.

2. The business world is a jungle. Research and understand that jungle in its entirety. You have to know the market, the competitors as well as those who will try to destroy you.

3. Not only do you have to offer what people want, you have to offer it in a unique way; a way that your competitors do not. This uniqueness may reside in your product or service, the way it's delivered, or perhaps in your pricing. Marketing is critical!

4. Look into the future. While you are doing that, research exhaustively, getting to know the trends and where your niche is. And never stop researching

because you will want to be able to forecast, as best you can, future trends. Find the gaps!

5. Have a GPS plan: This involves planning every step and detail. Plan down to the penny and the minute, knowing exactly where you are going and what it will cost in dollars as well as in time. Without a plan, you will lose before you even get started.

6. Do the math. Every penny counts, and there is no room for error, especially when you are competing with the "big boys." Simple miscalculations can be costly. And don't fudge your own numbers with unreasonable expectations or underestimated costs.

7. Whether you opt for smaller volume with higher prices or large volume and lower prices, know your profit to the penny. Further, know where every penny is going. There is a great Italian saying: *L'occhio del padrone ingrassa il cavallo,* which means the eyes of the owner will fatten the horse; tend to your business with great care and detail and you will be rewarded with a fatter profit margin.

8. When plotting your budget to the penny, always consider the "screw-up factor." You will inevitably run into one problem or another, so leave room in your budget for it. Many make the mistake of not anticipating glitches or screw-ups. A flooring tradesman, for example, will always order ten

percent more flooring than a job requires to allow for waste and screw-ups.

9. Acquire the ability to read and completely understand financial statements. When dealing with investors, bankers, shareholders or partners, you have to be able to put together financial plans and be able to read and understand them thoroughly.

10. Business is like a chess game; you always have to be five steps ahead. When you go to make your next move, calculate what you think your competitors may do. Consider your options and the moves you will make if, for instance, interest rates skyrocket or a recession comes.

11. Team, Team, Team. You must have a good team. It is said, "We are only as good as the people we surround ourselves with." Hard workers, smart people, and professionals in the field will all contribute to the creation of your plan and your success.

12. Make as many connections as you can; smart people can give good advice and powerful people who can help make it happen. Never underestimate the importance of connections. You can do in a phone call with a good connection what might normally take months or years to achieve.

Charlie Agro and I celebrating my Premo Abruzzo Award

Chapter Thirteen

UP CLOSE AND PERSONAL
with Peter

"There is always opportunity.
It's all about finding the gap and filling it." P.M.

When a few people got word that I was writing my story and offering my humble tips on leadership, success and happiness, they put forward some questions of their own. I have taken questions from a couple of those young entrepreneurs and answered them here. I hope they are relevant and helpful to you as well.

1. **QUESTION**: If you had to choose one, which is most important: having the right systems in place for a business or finding the right people?

   ANSWER: Both are of equal value but, if I had to choose, I would say that having the right people is more critical. The right team will develop the right systems. Having the right people in place is essential because they will not only put the systems in place, they will accurately forecast revenue and cost.

2. **QUESTION**: What is the greatest challenge to scalability (a business' potential to access more of the market in order to expand)?

   ANSWER: Your product has to be saleable to everyone or to as many people as possible. Identify the most successful business in the area you are getting into and model yours after what has already proven to be working well. Start with one location to see if it will work and, once you have mastered operations there, expand in your area. Do not reach out too far; grow first in the market and area you are already in. With a solid foundation in place, you can go further afield. Understand your market down to the smallest detail, paying particular attention to where the revenue is coming from and how your business is different and better than that of your competitors.

3. **QUESTION**: How important is it to protect your downside while growing your business? Is it better to be a gunslinger and go for the gold or to tread lightly and take care through the growth phases?

   ANSWER: Everything evolves around an excellent business plan. Map out, in great detail, how you will end up having one hundred branches. Fearlessness is really having confidence in yourself and your plan, believing it is better than your competitors'. Understand your own limitations: Before you become a gunslinger, you have to understand the frontier you are in and who it is you should be shooting at. Plan everything in your war room. Know your plan inside and out before you begin the war, and then you can decide how aggressive you want to be.

4. **QUESTION**: Do most successful businessman ultimately measure their success in profits or is there a more fundamental driver?

ANSWER: Unfortunately, everyone in this world judges others by their bank account. Yet, success is much more than money. You go into business to make yourself a better human being. People get so wrapped up in the money that they become slaves to their own greed. Inevitably, those people will become miserable. Success is about growing and becoming a better person. At the same time, making money is critical because the more money you make, the more people you can help.

5. **QUESTION**: Things have changed dramatically over the past fifty years. At one time, a handshake was better than a contract. It seems that you could trust people more back then. Do you find this to be true?

ANSWER: Unfortunately, that is correct. A handshake is no longer enough. People have become self-centred and greedy. There are exceptions but, generally speaking, be sure to have a contract. Everything has changed with employees, too. Today, they tend to move from one employer to another, so there isn't the trust or loyalty there once was. You must have business controls and processes in place to guide the moves the employees make. On another note, with the help of modern technology, you can run multiple businesses over your phone. With cameras and other technologies, you don't need to be running back and forth between locations in order to manage all the details.

6. **QUESTION**: It seems like everything has been done. Is it better to pick an industry and attempt to take over a part of its market share or to be innovative and try to reinvent the wheel or fill a gap somewhere else? I think many young people believe that all the gaps have been filled already. They can get discouraged thinking how difficult it is to break in.

   ANSWER: Young people may think all the gaps have been filled, but there are gaps out there that need to be filled. Inventors and entrepreneurs felt that way over a century ago when there were just one million or so patents. There is an infinite amount of room for new inventions and ideas. As long as people have needs and wants, there will always be room for new approaches, concepts and inventions. Look at well-established industries and inevitably you will find gaps. I have done this throughout my life – finding myself starting at new business opportunities because I spotted a gap that needed filling.

If the gap is not there, your gut will tell you it's not for you. Whatever product or service you decide on, get advice from experts and research it to death. You can be a shoemaker – but be the best you can be and fill the gaps that exist in that business. If you are going to make lasagna, make the very best in town and offer it at a price that meets the needs of the buyers. It's all about finding the void and filling the gap.

7. **QUESTION**: How do you balance being driven by making money and being driven by personal happiness?

    ANSWER: First, you should always do what brings you happiness. Don't bother wasting your time and energy doing something just for the sake of money. I think it is a life wasted if you go to work every day hating what you do. And success is much more likely when your heart and soul are in the work you do. At the same time, I recognize that most of the human population has to do work they don't like in order to provide for their loved ones. I admire these people. They work for the greater good, and they reap much happiness knowing that their sweat will provide their family with comfort and opportunity. It is a noble venture to earn an honest paycheque that puts food on the table.

Years ago, I was running many businesses. I had acquired the food and beverage services at golf courses and cafeterias in numerous government buildings, plazas and factories and was running weddings out of the legions and the RBG. All of this was in addition to Carmen's Banquet Centre. There were times I felt as if I was going crazy. I was making money and took great pride in making profits in places where others had failed, but it was taking a heavy toll on me. One day, my friend Max challenged me. He asked me, "Why are you doing all this and driving yourself insane? I bet that if you focused solely on your banquet centre, you would make the same or more money." Max's words kept ringing in my ears until I finally decided to heed his advice. I sold everything else and focused on the banquet centre. As it turns out, Max was right. I regained my sanity and made more money from just running the banquet centre. I became more creative and had my best year ever. I was much happier, too.

This story may answer your question from a business perspective yet there is something much more important here: Running all these businesses took away time I could have spent with my family. I was neglecting the most important part of my life. In the madness, I lost sight of that part of life that is the most important; the part of life that brings us the greatest happiness. We all live with regrets, and this has been one of my greatest regrets. I should have spent more time with my wife and three children. Hopefully, I can make up for some of that with the time I now spend with my grandchildren. To my young readers out there: Always put your own happiness and the happiness of your loved ones ahead of making a buck.

Gerry Dee and Mayor Fred Eisenberger at another Charity of Hope fundraiser

Chapter Fourteen

HAPPINESS and the SPIRITUAL LIFE

"Keep your heart and mind pure with Jesus as your friend. When you stray, it will bring misery to you and your loved ones." P.M.

I'm certainly no expert to speak about philosophy or theology. Yet, since the beginning of time, people have sought happiness and the spiritually enlightened life. So many great thinkers have written on this topic. Who am I to speak on these topics? However, the writer of this book believes I have valuable things to say, so I offer my humble thoughts. I hope you find them helpful.

Before I present my personal formula for happiness, I believe that happiness is subjective. What brings happiness to one person can be slightly different than what brings happiness to another. However, there are universal principles that apply to all people. These principles or values are what I present to you here. To define a state of happiness, true happiness, is somewhat of a challenge. I believe I can best sum it up by saying happiness is achieved when one attains a state of mind that is filled with peace, contentment and enlightenment.

My ingredients for happiness are listed here and can be termed: **"LARGE."**

Love

You have all heard it said that money will not buy you happiness. It is said by so many people across time and around the world because it is true. Money can buy you a materially comfortable life, but money cannot buy you happiness. If we live life believing that money buys happiness, we will be constantly snarled by traps. When you get wrapped up in making money and stoking your own ego, you will lose sight of loving relationships. We are called to be a people who are loving, but it is difficult to love when our egos get in the way. Humility allows us to understand that there is something greater than us in this universe. The challenge is to rid oneself of ego and remain humble and loving. A saying that has helped me keep perspective is: "Think of death seven times a day, and it will keep you humble. But don't think of it all day or you will never get out of bed."

Your primary driving force ought to be bringing peace and joy to the people you love, to empower them and help them be better people. This applies to your family and friends as well as to your colleagues and employees. You cannot accomplish this if you put yourself before everyone else.

Attitude

We should all seek happiness; it is good for us on every level. The problem is we often look for happiness in the wrong places. We may be fooled into believing it can be found in drugs or alcohol, sex, gambling, power or material possessions. Like all of you, I walk the journey of life, each and every day learning something new. In my own search for happiness and the "good life," I have been misled and I have strayed. But I am fortunate to be able to say that, for the most part, I have lived what I would consider a happy and full life. I have been extremely blessed with having the freedom and God-given ability to make a living doing what I love. I have been the recipient of financial rewards beyond my needs and enjoyed a boatload of exciting experiences. I have been gifted with wonderful friends and relationships in and outside of my business. Most importantly, I was blessed with a wonderful wife, children and grandchildren. What more can anyone ask for than a loving family and people who accept your love with open arms and give you their love with open hearts?

I am so grateful for all of it. The critical ingredient here is gratitude. People with gratitude tend to be happy. You have to be grateful for it all – the good and the bad. Gratitude gives you the energy to get up every day with enthusiasm, to approach every day with a positive attitude and to draw out of any experience the good that can come from it. There will be many times in life when you are punched in the gut and you will fall. But, if you can pull the good and the lesson out of that experience, you will remain positive. Everyone wants to be around a person who has a great attitude. People are drawn to those who are always grateful. Gratitude brings cheerfulness; cheerfulness brings joy; and joy brings that state called happiness.

If you are a person of gratitude you will have the capacity to forgive people, even those who bring you harm. You cannot be happy if you have anger in your heart or you hang onto a desire for revenge. With forgiveness, you will see the best in the worst of people, and you will forgive them, setting yourself free.

Righteousness

As much as I have found peace and a fair share of happiness in my life, I believe that if I could go back and undo some of the things I did, I would be more content with the life I lived. It is impossible to be happy if you go against God's principles. He provides the path for us, and when we deviate from that path, misery moves in. I don't believe there is one path to happiness; each of us finds our own path in our own way. However, if that path deviates from that which is righteous and good, we will not be happy. Perhaps it is the poor that have a greater righteousness that we lack. Their hands are empty and this leaves lots of room for God. Our hands are so full there may be too little room for God's love and grace.

Being the person God has called me to be is what brings me happiness. You may wonder, "What does God call Peter Mercanti to be?" I believe He calls me to be righteous. Any regrets I have stem from moments in my life when I was not righteous. When I turned away from doing the right things and thinking the right thoughts, I lost any sense of real happiness. So, stay pure and close to God, keeping Jesus as your best friend.

Some people have asked me, "How can I be happy as a businessperson, succeeding in a cruel and hard business world?" Personal happiness cannot be separated from happiness in business. You can be a nice person and still do the right things in business. You do have to be tough, though, and never allow people to walk over you. You cannot sacrifice your integrity or be used as a doormat. There are many who will try to take advantage of these kinds of businesspeople but, if you think highly of yourself and have integrity, you will not allow such people to treat you this way. Being tough – not allowing people to take advantage of you, nor allowing them to compromise their own integrity – is being righteous.

Employees are happier and work harder if they are working for a person of integrity. Living the righteous and spiritual life motivates and inspires employees and allows for ideal team building. They will be happy knowing they work for someone who is righteous. With righteousness comes fairness, justice and prudence. When a business owner uses fairness and justice, it builds a culture of compassion and mutual respect. It creates a culture of happiness.

Running a business is a roller-coaster ride but, when you stay close to God, He will keep you strong and steady. Love, gratitude, generosity and righteousness will never have a negative effect on a business. It will never hurt the bottom line; in fact, it will increase your business success and profits.

Generosity

One of my trips abroad brought me to Dubai, a paradise paved in gold. Two hours after leaving Dubai, I found myself in the ghettos of Bangladesh. Ten people live in a one-hundred-foot hut in squalor. Yet, these people were happy. I discovered the same happiness in the poorest of the poor in Africa. The poverty disgusted me and caused me to wonder how the world ever got to this point. *Why do we live in such a world,* I wondered. *Why would the wealthy allow this to happen? Is it right that I return to a beautiful home, cars, a pool and a wealthy country?* I developed a great respect and admiration for those who devote their lives to fighting poverty.

I started to re-evaluate everything. I became sick with the thought of the amount of food that our company had wasted over forty years when I considered that thirty percent of the food we serve at an event is not eaten. It sparked in me a desire to do as much as I could to support charities through my business. And it redoubled my desire to help employees and friends going through difficult times. Getting back to happiness, it taught me that many of the poor, although they did not have economic happiness, found true happiness deep within. They were extremely generous, offering what little they had. It got me thinking that perhaps generosity is a critical ingredient to being happy. Not only were they generous with what little food they had, but generous with sharing their humble hut and their love.

What a wonderful feeling to be generous! More importantly, I worked hard on myself to be generous with my own love. I cannot help but conclude that generosity plays an important role in our happiness. No one can deny the wonderful "high" that comes from being generous with others.

Excellence

Never mistake excellence for superiority over someone else. And excellence truly can only be measured by you. Excellence is not about "measuring up" to society's expectations or living up to someone else's standards. Excellence is intimately connected to our pursuit of happiness and to our spiritual development because aiming for excellence will constantly push you forward to be better at your work but also in your relationships and your own personal development. Strive to be excellent.

Each of us knows deep inside what we are capable of doing, and all of us are capable of being great and doing great things. I'm not talking about being millionaires or achieving prestige in society. I'm talking about being the best you can be. I am always amazed and inspired by people who achieve excellence, whether they are servers, tradespeople, businesspeople or mission workers. The worst thing we can do is underestimate ourselves. I would consider it sinful to underestimate oneself and not use the great gifts one is given.

Whether it is a trade, a skill or your personality, whatever it is, strive for excellence.

The greatest degree of spiritual enlightenment and happiness comes to those who seek excellence in their thoughts, actions, work and character. Always seek excellence!

Ain't I lucky!

Chapter Fifteen

MY FAMILY

"You can make mistakes, fail and go bankrupt,
but if you have the love of your family and friends,
you are a rich man." P.M.

My Brother Sam

Everyone should have a guardian angel who looks out for you from the afterlife. We should also have a guardian angel in this world. My brother Sam has been my guardian angel in this life. He was my dad when my dad was not there. He has been my best friend, mentor and my rock. It started when we were kids when we would go out and hustle to make money, Sam saving every penny in a small piggy bank he made. Not only did he always look out for my best interests, he did the same for many family members, including his extended family. His commitment and love for family has always gone well beyond words, showing itself in his generous actions. He took care of many family members, helping many of them become millionaires.

Sam quit high school at the age of seventeen, eager to get to work and make his way into the business world. He went to work for Uncle Dino and his brothers who owned Mercanti Auto Refinishers at Strachan and Bay in the North End. The uncles then bought another auto body shop, Ontario Auto Collision, on Gage near Beach Road. Sam proved to be so brilliant at business (a gift he claims was passed on to him by Mom) that he quickly became a partner with the uncles. In 1972, at thirty-five years of age, Sam became President of Ontario Auto Collision.

The auto-body industry was known to be filled with dishonesty and corruption. Sam was determined to clean it up, always putting integrity above profits. He created an ethical approach at every level, his motto being: "Say what you do, do what you say, prove it and improve it." This is the ISO Model (International Standards Organization).

Sam managed to have such an impact on the industry that it gave him the credibility to purchase the CARSTAR franchise for Canada. He began with his main office on Rymal Road and grew to more than 300 locations across the country. Sam was also instrumental in making Carmen's a great success, dating all the way back to when he got our first loan from BMO for Carmen's Bakery.

Sam's generosity has extended beyond family and friends to helping those around the world. He on the board of directors for St. Joseph's hospital for twenty-three years as well as starting the Charity of Hope, with branches now open in Brantford and Oakville, too. He has raised over $2 million for his charity and has donated a small fortune to other charities over the years.

In spite of all his good works, Sam has had to deal with a lot of obstacles in his life, including jealousy and greed from others, even from those close to him. However, being the strong Christian man that he is and having a great capacity to forgive, he has always handled every situation with grace. For being such a wonderful human being, Sam has been blessed in so many ways; most of all by having such a wonderful wife, Roma, and three beautiful daughters – Lisa, Jenifer and Samantha.

My, my. What Sam and I looked like in the 1960's!

My Brother Morris

Morris was always viewed as our "little brother," despite how fiercely competitive he always was. He was a great and tough-as-nails athlete, an extrovert with a dynamic personality and a remarkable negotiator. There is a saying in business that goes something like, "It's not what you deserve, it's what you negotiate." Morris was such a great negotiator that he was nicknamed "The Edge." His company name became Edge Hospitality.

Sam and I would bring Morris with us when we sold newspapers and flowers. Although he was the youngest, he never looked to us to fight his battles. He could stand his own ground. His athletic abilities and toughness were always on full display, winning him a "C" championship in handball and causing him to excel in every sport he played. When he played football for Cathedral High School, he would run full speed, head-on, hitting anyone in his path like a cement truck. He was fearless.

1985 Handball. Great brotherly competition at the YMCA

The way Morris was in sports is the way he was in life, facing every challenge and obstacle head-on. He went on to graduate from McMaster with a Physical Education degree and secured a teaching position in a high school. Morris was our partner in the business, juggling Carmen's and his career as a teacher. A hustler and a "go-getter," he had the stuff to manage two careers and contribute greatly to Carmen's success.

Around the age of twenty-five, Morris was confronted with his greatest challenge. He and I played in a softball league at Victoria Park. We noticed that during a game, he would have difficulty breathing when he rounded third base. He later discovered he had cancer. The prognosis was not good. He was told to expect to live a short life and that he would never be able to have children. But, being the fighter that he was, Morris lived until the age of 61 and had three beautiful children: Marisa, Michael and Marcello. His wife, Lynn, has always been a warrior for Morris.

I bought out Morris from Carmen's Banquet Centre, and he was happy with his share, which was Oakville Conference Centre of Carmen's, including the Oakville Banquet and Conference Centre along with other venues. Today, Lynn does a great job running this company.

Throughout Morris' life, Lynn was always there, by his side every step of the way. Towards the end, after living in pain for thirty years, he was ready to surrender. Always being a man of faith and close to God, my brother was willing to let go and accept the limits of his earthly life. Although we can never enjoy another fun-filled evening with Morris and never be uplifted by his infectious smile, his love lives on in our hearts.

My mom and brother Morris ready to devour Mama Yolanda's Lasagna

My sister, Rosie

I was eleven when we were surprised with our miracle sister, Rosie. We didn't even know that Mom was pregnant. We called her the miracle sister because she was born prematurely, weighing just one and a half pounds. We always considered Rosie as our baby sister and, although we were not around a lot, we were always protective of her.

Of the four children, Rosie was the closest to Mom and Dad. Although she was born in Canada, she learned to speak Italian and to cook. Thanks to Mom, Rosie became an amazing cook, coming close to matching our mother.

Rosie attended Bishop Ryan and she was as good a student as she was a daughter and sister. She never caused any problems (unlike her brothers). She married John Lascala later in life because she would not settle for just anyone. In addition, John was the only man who was not afraid of Sam, Morris and I. We have all been blessed with their two beautiful children: Giuliana and Erica.

All her life, even while raising her own family, Rosie always remained closest to our parents. We have always had a great degree of gratitude for Rosie who took care of Mom and Dad as they aged and became ill. We were so involved in our business that we could not devote the time that Rosie could. The depth of her love has shown itself throughout her entire life, especially when Mom and Dad needed a lot of care.

Rosie has so many wonderful qualities, being a great wife, mother and human being. I believe her most outstanding quality is her kind heart. She radiates kindness. Perhaps she acquired that virtue from Mom. We live in a world that does not speak of kindness, let alone value it. It's as if that word has been dropped from the English language. Yet, it has to be one of the finest qualities a human being can possess, and Rosie has enough of it for the whole world.

My Daughter Daniella

Passionate, feisty, strong-minded and very attractive! Daniella is a clone of me only in female form (but I can only wish I had her looks). Sometimes, when two people are a lot alike, as Daniella and I are, it can be like oil and water. We have had our knock-out battles, with her usually winning. As I get older, I look back on the years with my beautiful daughter, and I have come to better understand my own stubbornness.

It doesn't matter much who is right when a father and daughter disagree on things because, when the daughter has her mother on her side, the father is sure to lose every time. Daniella certainly inherited my better qualities and managed to escape the worst of me. Like me, she will fight for what she believes in and never gives up, whether in her personal or business life. She is beautiful inside and out and has definitely inherited her grandmother's and mother's kindness.

I was present at her birth and remember wondering – as I looked at our beautiful newborn daughter – how anyone could not believe in God. How can you go into the hospital as two human beings and come out as three? The only answer is there must be a God! Daniella's birth increased my sense of urgency to become a good provider. It heightened my sense of responsibility and gave me the drive I needed to be successful.

Daniella grew to be a very attractive young woman. One time when we had gone on a trip to New York City and taken a long walk, she caused two traffic accidents. Men just could not drive by and keep their eyes on the road. They had to look back, causing two rear-end collisions. In addition to her physical beauty, she has an academic and bright mind, earning a Bachelor of Arts from McMaster University in Economics and a Masters of Education.

Daniella married a wonderful man, Chip, who is now my business partner and best friend. He is an outstanding businessman as well as a man of great character. Daniella is Chip's right arm in the running of their business, Mulas Construction Ltd. She assists Chip in running their business and is good at everything she does. They have given Gabriella and I three beautiful grandchildren: Nick, Marco and Francesco.

When I look back on my life, I realize what a blessing Daniella has been. She has been a wonderful older sister to her brothers and is a loving and compassionate mother to her boys. My life would never have been the same without her.

Proud dad giving away his daughter

My Son PJ (*Peter Joseph*)

PJ excelled in everything he did. It was evident from the time he was small that he was determined to excel. His love of sports showed when he went to St. Thomas More High School and played on the school football and hockey teams. He was also a straight-A student who got involved in extra-curricular activities, including being President of Student Council and a student trustee. PJ proved to have a good mind and be determined and a very hard worker. Being self-motivated and having such a strong drive to excel set PJ apart from others.

Different universities pursued PJ, and I had hoped he would attend a local Canadian university, but he was insistent on attending the University of Notre Dame in Indiana. I remember him writing me a three-page letter and attaching the poem "The Road Not Taken" and leaving it on my bed, making his case to attend Notre Dame. It brought me to tears. His letter was so powerful that

I would have dug ditches to make the money to make his wish come true. We visited Notre Dame, and I fell in love with this spectacular Catholic university.

While walking around the campus, we got lost and a priest stopped to ask us if we needed help finding our way. We got to talking and, when he discovered we were from Hamilton, he began telling us all about our city. When I asked him how he knew about Hamilton, he replied, "I am a priest; I know everything." He went on to explain that many of the Notre Dame priests were trained in Welland, Ontario.

As we crossed the border into Canada on our way home, I was going through the numbers in my head, calculating the cost given the Canadian dollar was worth sixty-two cents American at the time. It would be an expensive education, but I was comforted by the thought that PJ, a son of an immigrant father, would prove that he could compete with the best of them. No matter the cost, it would be worth it to give PJ what he wanted and the fine education he deserved. PJ excelled at Notre Dame, graduating with a degree in finance and economics and summa cum laude. It was the best investment I made in my life.

One of PJ's accomplishments was making his father a fan of the Fighting Irish, Notre Dame's football team. I attended some of their games with as many as 80,000 fans. On two occasions he had the honour to speak to 17,000 people at Notre Dame pep rallies.

PJ married a wonderful woman, Diana, and they have given Gabriella and I two precious grandchildren: Matthew and Gloria, with one more on the way. PJ has been a part of Carmen's since he started his working career, holding all kinds of jobs, learning every aspect of the business. He proved himself over and over to be capable of running a big business. An example of his competence and vision was his insistence on building our very successful hotel next to the banquet centre. Today, I am so proud to tell others that PJ and Joey now own and operate Carmen's Group.

My Son Joey

My wife's and mother's kindness travelled through the family like a warm breeze, crossing the face of all her grandchildren and injecting them with this wonderful virtue. Joey was certainly the recipient of this beautiful trait and he has demonstrated it throughout his life. His fine character and nature makes me proud of him every day. Because I was absent from home for so many years, working day and night, I feel as if I missed out on spending time with my children, relishing their beautiful qualities as they developed, especially Joey's kind soul and brilliant mind.

We named our first son Peter, so I made a promise to my father that our second son would take his name. When Gaby was pregnant with Joey (Joseph), I knew it would be a boy. It made my father very happy to have our second son named after him.

I loved watching Joey play senior football for St. Thomas More. He was a running back and, in one particular game, he created one of the most spectacular make-Daddy-proud-moments when he broke five tackles and ran for a 70-yard touchdown. It was one of two touchdowns he scored that day to win the city championship. He was recruited by universities to play football only to be curtailed by an injury.

Like PJ in many ways, especially in his drive to excel, Joey earned his black belt in karate. Even when I watched him break his nose in a tournament, I was proud to see him get back up again. Joey was also Student Council President and an excellent student. It's not athletic feats or scholarly accomplishments that make me so proud of my children. What makes me truly proud is the character of my children. Joey is always so loving and demonstrates kindness and caring toward everyone. He especially shows this as a husband to his wonderful wife, Rachel, and as a proud father to his three beautiful children: Joseph, Savannah and Evangeline.

In the area of business, Joey is especially gifted in electronics and is our go-to guy for all things technological. He has a brilliant mind for technology. His IT abilities have been a gift to Carmen's. If Carmen's did not exist, it wouldn't surprise me if Joey got a job with Apple or Google in Silicon Valley. These gifts of his have played a big part in ensuring success in the opening of the hotel. While working on the hotel and raising his family, he earned his CHA from Cornell University. He regularly visits all of our locations, making sure everyone is following corporate protocols.

Joey and PJ make the perfect business team. The bond between them is powerful, and they complement each other like yin and yang. They perfect each other's gifts and talents. The love between them and the way they think of each other, care for each other and support each other is enough to bring a father to tears.

There are so many families that don't get along – parents fighting with children and siblings fighting with each other. I have been truly blessed to be part of a family that is not like that. Even when I have done wrong and have hurt them, they have come to my rescue. It looks like the beautiful traits of love and kindness from my parents will be passed down for generations to come. I am so proud to be the father of these three wonderful people.

2020. Vineland Estates. PJ's fortieth birthday with Joey and Rachel, Daniella and Chip, PJ and Diana

My Wife Gabriella

Life is filled with magical moments that we never forget. The first time I cast my eyes on Gaby on that bus ride to school was one of those magical moments. Her beauty and aura captivated me, and I knew from that very first moment that this was the woman for me. The second magical moment, again on the bus ride, was sitting beside her and kissing her on the cheek.

Our band was booked to perform at a dance at All Souls Church. Prior to the performance, I wrote a song called "I Love You, Yes I Do" with Gaby on my mind. Knowing Gaby would be at the dance, I performed it for her and made a point of casting my attention her way as I sang. I introduced the song by saying, "The next song goes out to a very special person, and you know who you are."

Gaby and I started to date, going to a show at the Tivoli Theatre on James North, followed by a meal at the Tivoli Restaurant. Every time I was with Gaby, it was magical. My friends and family loved her – not just because she was a head-turner, but because of her kind and gentle nature. I was grateful to have her parents, Stephania and Libero, accept and like me, and my relationship with her parents grew into a strong friendship over the years. I was also grateful that her two very gifted and athletic brothers, Eddie and Claudio, also accepted me into the family. Libero and Stephania were very hard-working people and they loaned me money when I was starting in the business world.

Gabriella and I got married and had our reception at Luso Canadian Hall on James North, hosting five hundred people, not counting the friends who were not invited but couldn't stay away. When we moved to the Mountain, Gabriella's father came to me and told me that he and his wife wanted to be near their daughter. We helped them find a home nearby so that they could remain close to their daughter and grandchildren.

Gaby was young when Daniella was born. Ten years later, we had PJ and then Joey. Gaby has been my rock throughout my entire personal and business life. Because of the demands of my business, I was like an absentee father for many years. I never worried about the children because Gaby was the best mother a child could hope for. She not only supported me in all my decisions and in business, she was the source of emotional and spiritual nourishment for the children. Gaby is an angel, to this very day, who never stops doing for the family. In addition to looking out for and supporting our children, she is constantly caring for the grandchildren, always cooking and buying them clothes.

Every marriage goes through difficult times. Nobody is spared the suffering of obstacles and difficulties. But the love of family and the love of a spouse can overcome and outlast any problem. This love, combined with vows to be true to each other in good times and bad, in times of sickness and health, when finances are good and not so good, and to do it "until death do us part," can give any couple the strength of character to overcome even the toughest obstacle. I love Gaby today as much as I ever have.

"Beauty and the Beast." She always made me look good.

Every day that passes, I appreciate her goodness more and more. She is kind, caring, strong-minded, thoughtful and beautiful. Fifty years later, Gaby remains my rock and always will be. The song I wrote and sang to her, that night at the church hall over fifty years ago, still applies to how I feel about her today:

I LOVE YOU, YES I DO

If I say I love you baby, and you say to me you care
That's when I get your hand, and me and you will walk the isle
Cause baby

I love you, yes I do, and I want you
I love you, yes I do, and I need you
I love you, yes I do, and I want you to be mine

When a man loves a woman deep inside
He sees the need for love
And I'm glad that you understand when I say to you
I care

And baby
I love you, yes I do, and I want you
I love you, yes I do, and I need you
I love you, yes I do, and I want you to be mine.

Your eyes looked, my eyes saw
And baby, baby, there we were in love
Then I knew that you and me were meant to be
That we were meant to be

And baby
I love you, yes I do, and I want you
I love you, yes I do, and I need you
I love you, yes I do, and I want you to be mine.

When a man loves a woman deep inside
He sees the need for love
So, c'mon baby take my hand
Me and you we'll walk the isle

So baby
I love you, yes I do, and I want you
I love you, yes I do, and I need you
I love you, yes I do, and I want you to be mine.

Now listen baby
Everything I said to you
I really meant with all my heart
I'll care for you, I'll love you
And I'll make you my everlasting moment
So listen to what I got to say.

I love you, yes I do, and I want you
I love you, yes I do, and I need you
I love you, yes I do, and I want you to be mine.

Woo Woo baby
Woo woo woo
I love you and I need you
Woo woo
I understand, I'm your loving man.

My Extended Family

As you may recall from my business model, I view teamwork as a critical component to success. The team you build will often extend beyond family to include friends, colleagues, associates and employees. Without a great team, it's almost impossible to succeed. I've been very fortunate to be surrounded by so many wonderful people throughout my life and career. All of them have contributed to our success. In addition to those I have told you about in my story, I want to take the opportunity to talk about others, sharing thoughts on some and giving special mention to others. I refer to them as my extended family.

Dennis Concordia

I met Dennis when we first opened Carmen's Bakery. He ordered a cake from us and, unfortunately, we made a mistake with the cake. He returned to point out our error. Ever since then we have been the best of friends. Dennis worked in management in the Marketing Department at *The Hamilton Spectator*. While carrying on with his career at *The Spectator*, he played a key role in my life, serving as my business and personal advisor, and continues in that role to this day. He also played a major role in my brother Sam's CARSTAR organization, acting as senior vice president.

I brought Dennis with me when it came time for me to purchase my crypt in the mausoleum. As we were looking for the right location on the wall, Dennis suggested that I should pick one that was eye level. I didn't like that idea. I explained to him that everyone is taller than me and I have been looking up to others all my life. Having my crypt high would be a great opportunity for me to have people look up to me when they visit. I picked out a crypt a few feet above my eye level.

Dennis also acted as the co-ordinator for special events, dealing with agents and celebrities, taking care of every detail and guaranteeing success with each event. Thankfully, he is still involved with the Carmen's Group. He is a rock-solid, no-nonsense guy who calls it as he sees it. What a great gift God gave me when he introduced me to Dennis.

Frank DeNardis

The annual festival called Festitalia continues after forty-five years. Frank DeNardis served as one of the first chairs and stayed on the board to connect the festival to the local media and business worlds. Frank was sent to New York City to learn his craft and eventually became general manager of CHCH Television. I'm proud that Carmen's became a very big part of the growth of the annual celebration of Italian art, culture, faith and food. I was proud to be a part of these celebrations and a supporter of Festitalia. I want to thank Frank for all he did and for being such a wonderful friend.

Henry Merling

I first met Henry Merling when he was Alderman for Ward 7 in Hamilton. He came into the bakery and introduced himself. From that first meeting we became friends and remained so throughout our lives. Henry was my personal friend as well as my "go-to" guy when I needed to work with city hall. Henry first showed me the land that Carmen's is built on. He strongly recommended I buy it, believing this remote area would grow. Henry immigrated to Canada with nothing and became one of Hamilton's most powerful politicians. I am infinitely indebted to Henry, not just for contributing to my success but also for being my decades-long dear friend.

Charlie Agro

As a teenager, Charlie was a good friend to my son PJ. My son brought Charlie in to help with the business. Charlie, while he was in school and then later when he became an educator, would come in on weekends. He was always on time and eager to work. We formed a strong bond working together and as friends. Charlie is very astute and never afraid to get to work. He is the best captain's soldier one could have on their team; loyal and hard working, dedicated and a great support to everything Carmen's.

Charlie added value to our business, especially when we hosted celebrity events where he would take on the task of formulating robust event programs to support the charity and event budget. He would be our go-to guy when we needed to solicit the community for funds by placing local business ads in the event program.

JC Campos

An expert in marketing, I refer to JC as my "Portuguese Prince." JC has a super personality and radiates kindness. I think I am drawn to people who are kind because kindness always reminds me of my mother. He has a wonderful personality and does not have a mean bone in his body. JC runs the entire marketing aspect of Mama Yolanda's Lasagna Company. His excellent communication skills, strong work ethic and dynamic personality certainly contribute to our success.

Steve Rydtschenko

Steve has a very challenging job as our executive chef, maintaining our secret recipes and guaranteeing consistency. He is a disciplined, no-nonsense chef who commands respect. As kind as he can be, if Steve tells you to do something, you had better do it. Steve was executive chef at other companies and has been around the world. We are happy and grateful to have Steve at Mama Yolanda's.

The Hon. James R.H. Turnbull

I met Jim during our handball days at the YMCA. Jim was a fantastic player. Jim is very close to my brother, Sam, belonging to the same bible groups. He is a superb human being and lives his life as a true Christian. He is always willing to offer me and others his wise and prudent advice. Jim raises a lot of money for charities and is very involved with the Joy and Hope of Haiti. He is a strong supporter and advocate of all things that help others.

Tony Perri

Tony was a lifelong friend, dating back to our teen years. Being short, people didn't think he could run fast. He would take bets and win every time. His short legs moved like the wind. Tony had an infectious personality that you could not help but love, always smiling and dynamic.

Tony had the exclusive DJ contract with Carmen's, and it was a pleasure to have him work at Carmen's in this capacity. Gaby and his wife Claudette have been friends for decades, and I am grateful to have had Tony as my friend. He was a very proud father to his son and daughter. Tony will be missed by many people.

Frank Calabrese

My friendship with Frank also dates back to our teen years. He was the organist in our band, Indigo. We continue to keep in touch and what a wonderful blessing it is to have friends for a lifetime. Frank is a true friend and a man filled with passion and love for everyone.

Frank's wife Lynn and Gabriella also remain close friends.

Joe Trombetta

Joe built an extremely successful mortgage business, Titan Mortgage. He has supported every event at Carmen's, taking a special interest in every event and the charities associated with them.

Joe would always find a way to help anyone find a loan or mortgage. If you were having problems getting a loan or mortgage, Joe was, and is, the man to call and see.

The Couture Family

Mario, Andre, Jerry, Nelson and John "Giggy" Couture were a very well-known family. All five brothers were extremely talented. John, nicknamed "Giggy", played for the Montreal Alouettes and was a pretty good boxer. They are a wonderful family of men and to this day, Andre is involved in my brother Sam's bible studies group.

Elda Faiella

Elda Fiella is a friend of thirty-five years and the face and voice of the Abruzzo association and community in Hamilton. She has organized an endless number of events and is a wonderful and beautiful Italian from our part of Italy, Abruzzo. Elda is one of the kindest, most passionate people I have met, keeping the Abruzzo association active and vital.

John Romanov

John is an exceptional architect who has been a dear friend since 1986. John designed Carmen's Banquet Hall as well as the Hotel. He is now designing our lasagna company. He is a very talented man who dresses better than any thirty-year-old, earning the nickname "Hollywood architect."

Tony Battaglia

A developer who started "Tradeport," what is now the Hamilton Airport, Tony was a wonderful friend and business associate. Unfortunately Tony passed away in January 2021. He has always been a great supporter of our special events. He is a class act!

Charles Juravinski

This is a man whose life story would inspire anyone. He faced and conquered many obstacles and ended up on top. I admire him and his wife, Margaret, for doing the most honourable thing – giving away most of their fortune to the hospitals.

Nick Bontis

Nick is a highly intelligent academic who teaches at McMaster's DeGroote School of Business. He lectures all over the world and is a pleasure to know. Nick has been involved with Carmen's Group for many years, and I'm proud to say he is my favourite Greek person. Nick is also a soccer enthusiast, closely working with his two sons, assisting them to develop into great soccer stars.

Tony Valeri

Tony is a special friend to our family and a big supporter of all things Carmen's. He has always been there for me and for our company, on a personal as well as a business level.

Fred Losani

One of our area's most accomplished commercial and residential builders, Fred was always supportive of Carmen's special events. I'm honoured to have him as my friend.

Judy Marsales

Judy has been a great success with her real-estate brokerage, offering professional and ethical services to their clients. Judy has been a strong supporter of Hamilton and its events, always supporting charities and especially the arts.

Justin Joseph

Justin was always an important part of our life, being PJ's best friend at an early age. He was always supportive of all things Carmen's, and to this day, he has remained a part of the Mercanti family, always attending our family gatherings and special occasions. I look forward to continuing our lifelong friendship for many years to come.

Michael Lamont

Michael is a very successful personal injury lawyer, advocating for victims of injustice. He is a major supporter of many local charities and organizations.

The DeSantis Brothers

Tony, Peter and Aldo are all from Abruzzo. The DeSantis brothers have had a significant and positive impact on the development of this great city in both the commercial and residential sectors. It has been a pleasure to know them and to work with them on a number of charitable events through Carmen's.

Joseph Mancinelli

Joe is the International Vice President of the Labourers' International Union of North America for central and eastern Canada, representing 800,000 members. Joe has been involved in many redevelopment initiatives in Hamilton's downtown core and has supported all of the charity events hosted at Carmen's.

Lincoln Alexander

Lincoln was a lawyer who became the first black Member of Parliament, Cabinet Minister, Chair of the Workers' Compensation Board and Lieutenant Governor of Ontario. Lincoln was such a great man, and I thank him for all his good work and support. We had the honour to host his eightieth birthday celebration at Carmen's.

Mario Nesci Sr. and Jr.

Mario Nesci Sr. has always been a strong supporter of Carmen's many fundraising events. It has been a pleasure and honour to know father and son and to work with both. I look forward to exploring future business opportunities with them.

Thomas J. Weisz

Tom Weiss of Effort Trust came to our rescue when we booked former vice-presidential candidate Sarah Palin for a fundraising event. When controversy erupted and supporters started to back out, he stepped up to help. He saved the day. Tom is a pillar in the community, always supportive of charity events.

Angelo Mosca

Hall of Famer Angelo Mosca played with the Hamilton Tiger-Cats from 1962-1972 and was named a five-time all-star. He played in nine Grey Cup games, helping to win five of them. He was viewed as the meanest player in the CFL and Mosca promoted his mean image when he entered professional wrestling as "King Kong Mosca." Although I once beat Ang in an arm-wrestling match, very few, myself included, could match his toughness. We honoured Ang at Carmen's with a packed event we called "Still Mosca." Ang certainly contributed to Hamilton's reputation as being a tough, gritty town. In 2015, his jersey, #68, was retired.

Ron Foxcroft

Ron Foxcroft is a great man who sponsors many charities and is known for being a man of gratitude, never forgetting to say, "Thank you." As a world-class basketball referee, he got frustrated on more than one occasion with the pea sticking in his whistle. This led Ron to invent the world-famous Fox 40 whistle that "Never gets stuck!"

Ron has always been a true ambassador for Hamilton, loving his city and locating his companies here; Fox 40 International and the Fluke Transportation Group. I am grateful for all the support and friendship Ron has given me and all he has done for our great city.

Craig Dowhaniuk

Craig held a prominent position in Hamilton and used his influence to bring the most iconic, world-renowned people to Hamilton, including Margaret Thatcher, Bill Clinton, George Bush, Sophia Loren, Mario Cuomo and many others. A special thank you to Craig for all he has done.

Natalia (Gabriella's aunt), Valerie, Laura and Jessica

Natalia is ninety-nine years old, but no matter how old she is or how far away her and her family lives, they have always stayed in touch and been a tremendous help to our family through their love and support.

Cora and John Miszuk

Cora and John were treasured neighbors on Elena Crt. And remain life long friends to Gabriella and I.

What a joy to know these wonderful people; their kindness, great character and support to fundraising events at Carmen's always exceeded our expectations. John was the first Polish born NHL'er and played in the NHL for years. They are the proud owners of several Tim Horton's franchises in Hamilton. Gaby and I couldn't ask for better friends and neighbors.

Roberta and Paul Said

When we started our seniors' shows at Carmen's, Roberta and Paul were our most regular and consistent supporters. They would always purchase a couple tables of tickets and promote the shows. Roberta, always cheerful and happy, would go to great lengths to get all her friends and associates together to attend these shows. Roberta's daughter Janice founded a wedding show called "The Total Wedding Show" in Toronto, and it became a great success.

Eddie and Claudio Fernetti (Gabriella's brothers)

Eddie and Claudio, Gabriella's younger brothers, have always been such a wonderful source of love and support for Gabriella and the entire Mercanti family. Both Eddie and Claudio are super athletic and fitness enthusiasts, with Eddie still retaining the body of a young man. Claudio was always a UFC fan and was trained in Jiu-Jitsu by one of the famous Gracie brothers. He received his certification and opened the first school of its kind in Oakville.

David Lysecki

David has been one of my son Joey's closest friends since high school and continues to be to this day. David is Assistant Professor in the Department of Pediatrics at McMaster University as well as an Associate Member in the Division of Palliative Care, Department of Family Medicine at McMaster University. I encourage everyone to support David in his great work, working with the children of our country. He is a man with a great mind and a giant size heart.

Tony, Sue and Jessica DePaulo

Tony DePaulo has been one of PJ's closest friends since childhood. Unfortunately Tony passed away recently at a very young age. Tony's mother Sue and daughter Jessica have remained very close friends of Gabriella and Daniella.

Wendy and Mark Edwards

Wendy is the designer that made Carmen's and the hotel look as beautiful as it does. Wendy, Gabriella and Daniella have become great friends and often enjoy lunches together. Wendy is also the chief strategist, working with Daniella, in the decor of the many beautiful homes that Chip and Daniella have built in Hamilton and Ancaster.

Joe Fardell

During my years as chairman of the tourism board, Joe Fardell and I, along with our wonderful committee, had many dinners and lunches together strategizing on ways to attract more conventions to Hamilton. As a result, major events came to our great city. Joe is so intelligent that he was scooped up by the city of Calgary, working there for five years and then returning to Hamilton.

Frank and Maria Mulas

Frank and Maria are the parents of my son-in-law Chip. Prior to Chip and Daniella getting married, I was good friends with Frank and Maria. They were very supportive in the building of Carmen's and always remained great friends. Chip's brother Tony, his wife Anna and son Andrea have also remained very close to our family throughout the years.

Sam Malatesta

Sam is one of the most interesting people I have met in my life. Not only was he employed by Carmen's in his teen years, he also was instrumental in contributing to the success of CARSTAR. My most memorable experience with Sam was when he attended

McMaster University and held dances at Carmen's Banquet Centre. These events were extremely successful for both Sam and Carmen's. He now runs a very successful consulting company in the automotive sector.

Sergio Manchia & Matt Johnston
Owners of Urban Solutions

Over the years, Urban Solutions have closely worked with me and my son-in-law Chip on several development projects. Their professionalism and expertise is second to none and they have been an honour to work with. With their team of professionals, they are the "go to" company to secure any development approvals.

Mercedes and Javier,
Owners of Mercedes Salon and Day Spa

Gabriella and Daniella have been very close friends with Mercedes and Javier over the years. One of our most enjoyable trips was spending time with them in Spain for a family wedding. They are wonderful friends and great to spend time with.

Steven and Deborah Frankel

Steven is one of our family's lawyers and Daniella and Chip's close friend. Steven has always been a great friend, very protective of our family and keeping our best interests in mind throughout the years.

Virginia and Everton Moncrieffe

These two are the most loyal and supportive employees in the history of my company. Virginia started with us in 1993 and has literally done every job the company offers – server, receptionist, limousine driver, truck driver, inventory clerk, and event worker and now serves as my executive assistant. Everton joined us in 1990 and has done an outstanding job creating the most beautiful "set ups" for every event. He is responsible for every aspect of this job and is our Vice President of Building Operations.

My Neighbours on Mill Creek

Living on Mill Creek Court with my neighbours has been like a blast from the past. It reminds me of the way life used to be: families living in the same home for decades, a strong sense of community, forging strong friendships, celebrations on special days and socializing at every opportunity, people looking out for each other's children and now their grandchildren. What a wonderful place to live. I want to thank all my neighbours for playing a special role in my life and the life of our family. Thank you to: Paul and Patti Stever, Julien and Shirley-May Serena, Paul and Tracy Ferrie, Peter and Sandy Montour, Dr. Dominic and Tina Raco, Shik and Elka Patel, Tony and Judy Cipolla, Paul and Rita Giardini and my friend since we were teenagers, Paul Vaccarello and his wife Gina.

In addition to the people above, there are so many others who contributed in their own unique ways and with their own special talents. I take this opportunity to acknowledge them for all they have done for me and for the Carmen's Group:

Ammar Balika

Jack Pelech

Georgie and Ernie Moore (the former wrestler "The Executioner")

Brother Richard MacPhee

Cathy Wellwood

The Galli Family

Sonya and Doug Gilmour

Ang, Paul, Michael and Remi Paletta

Charlie Cino

Olga and Alex Teleghena

Louisa and Carmelo Iudica

Debby Russ

Shirley Lewis

Paul Zarycki

Fausto Capobianco

Donny D'Angelo

Andi Pojani and Kat Lamb

Matthew J. Abraham

Luana Heinbecker

Tony Tumolo

Angela Posteraro

Murray Van Der Marel

Mike Sienna

William and Irene Lowenhow

Pauline Ouellette

Jackie Cooke

Tracy Robinson

Albert and Mimosa Sholla

Darko Vranich

Chad Dixon

Louie DiDiomede

Steve McGuigan (Hamilton Tiger Cats)

Nino Bucci

The Pietrantonio Family

The Ventresca Family

The DiAntonio Family

Bob Young

Sam Merulla

David Lysecki

Michael Andlauer (Hamilton Bull Dogs)

The Miszuk Family

The Macaluso Family

Glen Gibson and Family

Nancy DiGregorio and Family

The Cortina Family

Peggy Chapman

Cathy and Stan Keyes

Fred Losani

Cecilia Carter-Smith

Jasper Kujavsky

Art Duerksen

Colin Millar

Emilio Mascia

One of our many sponsored golf tournaments

Chapter Sixteen

THE BEGINNING:
MAMA YOLANDA'S LASAGNA

"Life begins at 70!" P.M.

It's not as much about how you start the race as it is about how you end it. I want to end my race with a bang. In 2015, I was coming to the end of my business with Carmen's. I no longer was the physical man I used to be, able to scrap with giants and live up to my nickname One-Punch Pete. I was no longer the champion arm wrestler who beat the likes of Angelo Mosca, Hall of Famer football star Peter Dalla Riva and other Hamilton muscle men and even the best on Notre Dame University's football team. I was no longer the man who beat up three thugs who were harassing a loved one. I had eaten enough banquet food, run enough events and shaken enough hands to last ten lifetimes.

Coming to this stage in my life and wanting to see my children and grandchildren excel, I was willing to let it go. I sold the entire business to my sons, PJ and Joey. It involved Carmen's Banquet Centre, the Hotel as well as contracts with places such as Hamilton Convention Centre and Lakeview Confederation Park. Over the years, the boys had worked every aspect of the business and had the talent, skill, enthusiasm and work ethic to take over Carmen's and make it grow. They are both bright and hard-working young men, and I felt confident they would do a great job. I had no reservations about this decision and looked forward to watching them take the business to the next level. Having been the boss for thirty-five years, I knew I had to remove myself completely so I would not interfere with their vision and dreams.

2015. The old bull retiring. A new beginning!

In high school, Gabe Macaluso and I lived in the North End. It was a long bus ride to Scott Park High School in the East End of Hamilton and sometimes we would be late. On several occasions, we were sent to the principal's office for a scolding. On one occasion the principal told us, "You two guys won't amount to anything. You're at the bottom of the barrel."

I remember thinking to myself, *Gee, he could have said the middle of the barrel or the quarter of the barrel, he didn't have to say we are at the bottom of the barrel.* Many years later, Gabe became the head of HECFI and I had become a successful businessman. Gabe had to attend a school-board meeting, and he invited me to join him. Our principal from thirty years earlier, now a public servant, was also in attendance. When our former principal turned up after the meeting had begun, Gabe was quick to point out to him that he was late and reminded him of what he had said to us thirty years earlier. Gabe then made it clear to him – and to everyone in attendance – that we had both amounted to something. Following the meeting, the former principal apologized to both of us for what he said all those years ago.

When you have experiences like this or if you are bullied, it can make you angry, bitter and resentful. Or, it can motivate you to be successful and to become the best person you can be. For me, these experiences turned out to be blessings. They motivated me to excel and to set high standards. I was naturally competitive, inquisitive and full of energy. It was part of my nature to become my best possible self. Perhaps that is why I could never completely retire.

I still had that competitive spirit and strong work ethic, plus a lifetime of knowledge, hard-won wisdom and a creative spirit that would never allow me to just golf and belong to clubs. I was used to working seven days a week, eighty to ninety hours a week. I had to do something. Although my body told me I was seventy years old, my mind told me I was still thirty. I am an entrepreneur and will be until the day I die. I always have to be creating and building something. For myself, purpose and meaning is found in work. I don't think it is possible for someone like me to ever stop working. I have to get up every morning, thanking God for another day and looking forward to accomplishing something and perhaps, overcoming another challenge. When I asked myself, "What's next?" making my mother's lasagna available to the world was the obvious choice.

Daniella's husband Chip has been such a blessing in my life. I have grown to love him in every way. With Gabriella and I living with Daniella and Chip and their children, Chip has become my best friend. He is a man's man: smart, kind, thoughtful, respectful and a great husband and father. Chip was instrumental in the building of Carmen's Hotel. He runs his own business with caution and care. He is a gifted stone mason and a very artistic designer. Chip and I became partners in the pursuit of the next dream, Mama Yolanda's Lasagna. I could not pursue this dream without him.

Chip and I jumped on the opportunity to buy a piece of land on Upper James. We purchased the land with the intention of severing it. At the same time, we were experiencing a lot of success with Mama Yolanda's Lasagna, using a small space at the back of Carmen's as our manufacturing plant. We would direct our customers to purchase our product at Lococo's supermarket, who provided us with our own freezer bunker. It wasn't long before Lococo's, Bennett's, Nardini's, Sobey's, Foodland, Fortinos and No Frills started carrying our product. Our success has meant having to lease a bigger space to manufacture our lasagna. We found the right spot on Nebo Road. With the company growing fast, we may move one more time to an even bigger facility before we occupy our own lasagna manufacturing plant in a few years.

You may recall me sharing with you from my childhood that as poor as we were when we were in Italy and in Hamilton, we always believed we were doing okay because of the abundance of delicious food, presentable clothing and the great love that existed in our family. No matter how poor an Italian family is, they always find enough money to eat like kings. Life revolves around that kitchen table where we enjoyed great meals and wonderful conversation.

My education with food started when I was seven and, as you know, continued throughout my life. I was prepared to start a whole new career in the food industry. While living on Caroline Street I made friends with Leroy O'Connor, an Indigenous man. One day, like most days, my mother made me a beautiful sandwich for lunch, with prosciutto, provolone, tomatoes and other goodies on a nice crusty bun. I went to visit Leroy at his house, and he came out with a sandwich that his mother had made him for lunch. We studied each other's sandwiches and eventually agreed to switch, excited to bring our taste buds a new experience. His sandwich was peanut butter and jam. It tasted pretty good, but when I returned home and my mother saw me eating Leroy's sandwich, she asked me what had happened to the sandwich she had made me. When I told her, she grabbed me by the ear and gave me a gentle cuff to the back of my head. She then explained the difference in cost to make the two sandwiches and that I had been beaten in the deal. I learned that day, at seven years old, that when it comes to food, you had better know what you are doing and how to negotiate. I certainly continued to learn that over the next sixty-three years. I have come to know the food industry, how to negotiate and what constitutes good food. When contemplating my next career, at this young age of seventy, I had to go with my mother's lasagna.

Lasagna meant much more to me as a young boy than just nourishment. It represented many things, for instance, my mother's work ethic given the painstaking hours she spent in the kitchen to make wonderful meals, especially lasagna. She would roll out the sheets of dough, pound the beef and pork, make her own sauce from scratch and then put it all together to make something delicious. It also represented to me the perfect ingredients that she mixed together to be such a wonderful parent – mixing love, discipline, kindness, wisdom and life lessons into one perfect recipe. It represented those wonderful conversations and all the love shared around that kitchen table for so many years. That lasagna would come to represent thirty-five years of bringing joy to people from all over the world who walked through our doors at Carmen's. I started my life with lasagna and there is no better way to end my career than by providing the world with my mother's lasagna.

Chef (boss) Mama Yolanda and her helper, my father, Guiseppe Mercanti, making lasagna

Mama Yolanda's is taking off because people love my mother's lasagna. We are making money and the future looks bright. I think my mother, Iolanda, who watches over me from above, is proud of her son and happy to know the world is now enjoying her lasagna, a recipe that dates back seven generations. Eventually, Mama Yolanda's will join the Carmen's Group, and it will be part of the family business legacy for generations to come.

I would like to encourage you to be as loving as you can be, never lose focus of what is important, make the most of your own talents, pursue your dreams and Never Give Up! You will take a lot of punches in life and in the business world. Some will knock you flat. That's okay, just get up and keep on fighting. Your determination and self-confidence will bring you success, while striving to be righteous will bring you happiness. If someone hurts you or if you stray and do something that hurts you and the people you love, pray to Our Father, forgiving those who trespass against you – and try to forgive yourself, too. I wish you success and happiness in your life – and don't forget to keep your eyes open for Mama Yolanda's Lasagna. You'll love it!! After all, not only did the most famous and powerful people in the world love it, the Godfather himself (Al Pacino) had us ship it to his home in New York.

"God bless you all in your life and in the pursuit of your dreams." P.M.

Our first ever Sobey's store, Stone Church Road, Hamilton

(QR Code for Mama Yolanda's)